THE LAW OF MEDICAL LIABILITY

IN A NUTSHELL

By

MARCIA MOBILIA BOUMIL
Assistant Clinical Professor of
Community Health
Tufts University School of Medicine

and

CLIFFORD E. ELIAS
Professor of Law
Suffolk University Law School

ST. PAUL, MINN.
WEST PUBLISHING CO.
1995

COPYRIGHT © 1995 By WEST PUBLISHING CO.
610 Opperman Drive
P.O. Box 64526
St. Paul, MN 55164–0526
1–800–328–9352

ISBN 0–314–06660–8

 TEXT IS PRINTED ON 10% POST CONSUMER RECYCLED PAPER

 PRINTED WITH SOY INK

1st Reprint — 2001

To Syl and Janet

*

PREFACE

The need for a Nutshell book on medical liability appears to arise approximately every ten years. The first Nutshell book on medical malpractice was written in 1977 by Professor Joseph H. King, Jr. He expressed the view that the law of medical malpractice was, for many years, an esoteric field into which few ventured with confidence. He also expressed the hope that his book would remove some of the mystery. That first edition fulfilled his wish and presented a sense of order to a then complex field.

The second edition to that Nutshell book was published in 1986. It continued the effort to bring understanding and symmetry to the trends which developed since the date of the first edition. New areas had arisen, such as the broadened theory of informed consent. Some legislative reforms had been inaugurated, but it did not appear to stem the proliferation of malpractice actions.

Now, some ten years later, it has become apparent that another edition will not suffice. It has become necessary to write a new text in a field which has attracted enormous attention from the Congress, state legislatures, physicians and trial lawyers. The field has become identified clearly enough to warrant the inclusion of a variety of medical liability courses in the curricula of many law schools.

PREFACE

This Nutshell is not intended to cover every aspect of the field of medical liability. While its scope is narrower, the authors express the hope that law students and members of the legal profession will benefit from it. It has been written, as well, for health care professionals, such as physicians, legislators and administrators of hospitals and other health care organizations.

We are indebted to a number of individuals for their involvement in our endeavor. Suffolk University law students, in particular, provided us with research and writing assistance. Our deepest appreciation is extended to Kristin Bullwinkel, Mary Balsamo, Karen Fabiszewski, Amy Farrell and Matthew Kraunelis, law students who worked diligently for a period of two years, providing us not only with assistance, but also with guidance. Professor Elias's secretary at Suffolk, Melba Leyva-Hernandez, provided her usual high-quality skills, willingly and cheerfully.

While this is a new text, we wish to express our debt to Professor King for leading and illuminating the way.

MARCIA MOBILIA BOUMIL
CLIFFORD E. ELIAS

Boston, Massachusetts

OUTLINE

Page

OUTLINE

TABLE OF CASES

References are to Pages

TABLE OF CASES

*

TABLE OF STATUTES

TABLE OF STATUTES

TABLE OF STATUTES

*

THE LAW OF MEDICAL LIABILITY

IN A NUTSHELL

*

CHAPTER ONE

ESTABLISHING THE PROFESSIONAL RELATIONSHIP

I. IN GENERAL: NEGLIGENCE THEORY

Since much of medical malpractice litigation relies upon negligence theory, it is important to clearly establish the elements of that cause of action. The Restatement (Second) of Torts § 282 (1965) defines negligence as "conduct which falls below the standard established by law for the protection of others against unreasonable risk of harm." There are four major elements of the negligence action: (1) that an actor owes a duty of care to another; (2) that the applicable standard for carrying out the duty be breached; (3) that as a proximate cause of the breach of duty a compensable injury results; and (4) that there be compensable damages or injury to the plaintiff.

II. DUTY

In medical malpractice litigation the existence of a "duty" generally refers to an obligation of the defendant (whether he be a physician or other

1

health professional) to another individual (who is generally, but not always, his patient). The duty may refer to the physician's obligation to act or refrain from acting in a particular way; it may refer to the information that he communicates to his patient prior to acting; or it may refer to any of numerous obligations that a physician incurs upon entering into a professional relationship. It does, however, require that there be such a relationship, express or implied, before the applicable duty of care is owed. Thus a physician who declines to render care, and who has otherwise not undertaken to do so (for example, by previously agreeing to accept certain patients) is generally under no obligation and incurs no liability for failing to enter into a professional relationship.

Traditionally, at common law, there was a distinction between misfeasance (active wrongdoing) and nonfeasance (mere inaction). Misfeasance could be the subject of liability since the actor undertook an obligation and thereafter carried it out in a negligent manner, whereas nonfeasance would not subject the actor to liability because neither he undertook nor the law imposed upon him any duty to act or avoid injury. Thus the existence of a duty is critical to any negligence action, and failure to establish that element is generally fatal to a cause of action.

The duty of the medical practitioner is generally defined by the nature of the professional relationship. A specialist in one area may incur a duty to treat certain related conditions, but may have no duty to undertake treatment of other unrelated conditions, even if they are urgent or life-threatening. Similarly, an emergency room physician may have an obligation to treat anyone who presents himself for treatment in that setting, but on his way home incurs no liability for failing to stop and treat a passerby. In a free society individuals are not forced to undertake obligations which they decline to accept, as long as there is no implication of acceptance on the basis of an affirmative action. Like all other marketable services, the delivery of medical services is a voluntary undertaking and no requirement that any individual do so is generally imposed in the absence of a specific intention to accept it.

Although the existence of a physician-patient relationship is the hallmark of finding a duty of care, courts may, at times, be quick to find that a duty does, in fact, exist on the basis of the circumstances. As a result, most physicians will not decline to provide necessary services, particularly under emergency circumstances, so that some form of medical care is generally available to those who seek it. Even hospitals which, historically, could choose the patients they would admit and the circumstances of admission are constrained by numerous factors that today limit their discretion.

For example, those hospitals which receive any significant form of public assistance are forbidden from discriminating against potential patients on the basis of race, national origin or handicap. Those hospitals which received construction funds under the federally-sponsored Hill–Burton Act are prohibited from refusing to provide services to those unable to pay until a certain volume of free or reduced fee services has been rendered. In addition, certain statutory or constitutional provisions, as well as an institution's own charter, may affect admission practices, particularly for public hospitals. Thus as hospitals determine their own admission criteria, they need to be sensitive to numerous potential constraints which may limit their ability to select patients according to preference. In the event that a court finds that a patient was wrongfully denied services, the court will imply a duty of care, and hold the facility liable for whatever injury was proximately caused by the failure to act.

A. EMERGENCY CIRCUMSTANCES

This is not to say that most hospitals, particularly private entities, are not free to determine their own admission policies as long as they are not discriminatory. The major exception to this general principle pertains to emergency facilities and hospitals offering emergency care. As to those facilities, the general rule is that emergency treatment must be provided to anyone presenting an emergent situation. In some states this is required by local statute; in others it is imposed by licensing requirements or health regulations. Furthermore, in virtually all states the developing case law will impose a duty on emergency facilities to provide such services and make them available to anyone who presents himself in an emergency situation. There are two reasons for the imposition of such a duty. First, it is consistent with public health principles and codes for individuals requiring emergency services to be able to access the nearest emergency facility without jeopardizing their condition in seeking a more remote facility. Secondly, by indicating to the public that a certain facility offers emergency care, an individual in need of services will rely on being treated there and not lose valuable time going to such a facility, only to be turned away.

On the other hand, if a patient arrives in an emergent condition which a particular facility is utterly unable to handle because of the type of problem and the medical personnel available, the only duty that will likely arise (barring actual negligence in staffing) is due care in identifying the situation and preparing the patient for transfer to an appropriate facility. Courts are increasingly likely to impose a duty of care and hold an emergency facility liable for withholding treatment that could have been rendered if it results in further harm to the patient.

A hospital or other facility which provides emergency services to a patient who might otherwise be refused services does not necessary obligate itself to render further services once the patient is stabilized and the emergency passes. Thus the duty imposed by the emergent condition extends only so long as that condition exists. Once a patient is stabilized, an ongoing physician-patient relationship is not necessarily established which might require the physician or facility to provide follow up or other care. The implied duty that is imposed by the emergency is thus different than the obligation that arises in the context of a consensual physician-patient relationship.

B.   CONSENSUAL RELATIONSHIPS

A duty of care from physician to patient generally arises in the context of voluntary or consensual physician-patient relationship. An express (if not stated) agreement is entered whereby the physician agrees to provide treatment consistent with his abilities (generalist or specialist) and the patient's desire. The treatment is expected to meet a certain standard of care. The patient agrees to pay or arrange payment for the services and to generally cooperate with the treatment plan. It is important to note that even if the payment is reduced or the services are rendered free of charge, the same duty of care applies, as long as the physician-patient relationship is nevertheless consensual. Furthermore, even if there was not an express offer and acceptance for services to be rendered, courts may still imply that such a relationship existed by the totality of the circumstances.

What if a physician agrees to treat a patient but, after evaluation, changes his mind? The existence of a physician-patient relationship and the obligations that arise therefrom may depend upon the circumstances of the case. If, for example, an appointment is made some time in advance, and the patient presents the physician with a condition that is time sensitive (e.g., diabetes, which requires regular and periodic treatment), the physician is likely to be obligated to provide treatment or make an immediate and appropriate referral so that the patient's condition is not jeopardized in waiting for another appointment.

Suppose, instead, that an examination is made and the physician determines that the necessary treatment is beyond his capability or expertise? Referral to another physician is proper, and the initial practitioner should make sure that a suitable and timely referral is made. It is not appropriate, for example, to direct the patient to the American Medical Association for a referral; it is also not adequate to refer a patient to another practitioner who is unable or unwilling to treat the patient. On the other hand, a patient cannot refuse an appropriate referral, and thereafter insist that the referring physician continue to treat him on the basis of an ongoing duty.

Sometimes patients are brought to physicians in a condition that renders a voluntary or consensual relationship impractical. The patient may be unconscious, incompetent or otherwise incapable of manifesting an intent to enter a physician-patient relationship. In those cases the court may nevertheless be justified in finding the existence of a relationship, despite the lack of mutuality of assent. Indeed, the court may find that another person acting on behalf of the unconscious or incompetent patient entered into a physician-patient relationship. Such a relationship can either be implied-in-fact or implied-in-law. If, for example, a relative brings the patient in for treatment and expressly assents to services, a contract is said to be implied in fact. If, on the other hand, a patient is brought into an emergency room by police or rescue workers and in need of emergency services, assent to treatment is said to be implied in law. The patient, as a beneficiary of the "contract" between the person acting on his behalf and the physician, takes on the same rights and obligations as though as an express contract had been made. Moreover, both the physician and the beneficiary are entitled to enforce its terms.

Merely because a physician is consulted regarding a patient does not, however, subject the physician to the duties of a physician-patient relationship. A number of cases have addressed the issues of contacts made over the telephone. Whether or not a professional relationship results from such a contact depends upon the facts of the case. For example, if a patient telephones a physician in an effort to secure a diagnosis or treatment, and the physician undertakes to render such service, the court could conclude that a physician-patient relationship was established. See *O'Neill v. Montefiore Hospital* (N.Y.A.D.1960) (A physician who spoke to a patient over the telephone from an emergency room could have been found to undertake a physician-patient relationship). On the other hand, it is not a necessary result that merely consulting over the telephone obligates the physician to a duty of care.

Moreover, if a physician informally consults a colleague about a patient's condition, whether or not the patient is identified, the informal opinion is unlikely to result in a finding that a physician-patient relationship exists. See *Oliver v. Brock* (Ala.1976) (Informal consult in which primary physician recorded his conversation with a colleague in the patient's medical record did not give rise to a physician-patient relationship between patient and colleague). These cases must be distinguished, of course, from those involving an intended consultation or second opinion in which the consulting physician does establish a traditional physician-patient relationship.

Yet another situation was presented in *Giallanza v. Sands* (Fla.App.1975) where it appeared that a physician allowed his name to be used for the purpose of having a patient admitted to a hospital. The physician testified that he informed the staff that he would not be treating the patient; in fact, he had no contact whatsoever with the patient or her family. The court held that it was a triable issue of fact as to whether a physician-patient relationship had been created.

Notwithstanding the seeming willingness of courts to impose a duty of care arising out of a physician-patient relationship, there are some circumstances where courts draw the line. For example, in *Rainer v. Grossman* (Cal.App.1973), a medical school professor was sued by a patient who claimed that the professor had offered an opinion about a course of treatment after hearing about the patient's history. The appellate court upheld the trial court's dismissal of the action against the professor, stating that no physician-patient relationship could be established since the professor had no opportunity to control the actions of the treating physician. Furthermore, to hold otherwise would violate principles of academic freedom in which faculty members are encouraged to disseminate knowledge for the benefit of all.

C. DUTY TO NON–PATIENTS

While the presence of a physician-patient relationship is necessary to establish a duty on the part of the physician, it does not necessarily follow that once the relationship is found, it extends only to the patient. An obvious example is the physician who treats a pregnant woman and consequently incurs a duty of care to both mother and unborn child. In *Sylvia v. Gobeille* (R.I.1966), a physician neglected to prescribe gamma globulin for a pregnant woman after he knew she was exposed to German measles. As a result, her child was born with serious birth defects. The court held that a cause of action could be maintained by the child—a third party. In such a case, the plaintiff could probably plead a cause of action grounded upon both a third party beneficiary theory and an undertaking theory in tort based upon the treatment of the mother.

Duties to third parties, however, extend beyond the immediate duty to a third-party beneficiary. In *Shepard v. Redford Community Hospital* (Mich.App.

1986), a woman sought emergency care complaining of high fever, leg pain, congestion, headaches and weakness. She was diagnosed with a respiratory infection and discharged. Two days later, her son suffered from the same symptoms, and was hospitalized immediately. He died that same day after being diagnosed with spinal meningitis. In the wrongful death action that followed, the mother claimed that her misdiagnosis and improper treatment resulted in the death of her son. The claim was dismissed by the trial court on the basis that there was no physician-patient relationship between the doctor and the son, and thus no duty. However, the appellate court reversed, holding that the relationship between mother and physician gave rise to a "special relationship" which could result in a duty of care on behalf of the son.

Similarly, in *Bradshaw v. Daniel* (Tenn.1993), a patient was admitted to the emergency room with symptoms of the disease, Rocky Mountain Spotted Fever, and ultimately died of that illness only a day later. Although the physician communicated with the patient's wife, he never warned her that because of the circumstances under which the patient contracted the disease, she might also be at risk. The disease was not communicable, but both may have exposed to it at the same time. When she later came down with similar symptoms, and thereafter died of the illness, a suit was brought on her behalf alleging that the physician failed to warn her that she, too, might be at risk. The trial court dismissed the claim on the basis that there was no duty to warn a non-patient of the risk of exposure to a non-communicable disease. The Supreme Court of Tennessee reversed, however, concluding that the existence of the physician-patient relationship with the husband was adequate to impose an affirmative duty of care to warn persons in his immediate family about the risks concerning that illness.

There is also a line of cases beginning with *Tarasoff v. Regents of the University of California* (Cal. 1976), in which courts have considered the duty of a psychiatrist to third persons who might be injured by dangerous patients. In *Tarasoff*, the court found that a psychiatrist affiliated with the defendant should have known that his patient was dangerous and that an identifiable victim was the subject of his violent aggression. The court held that the physician had a duty to take reasonable steps to protect third parties, assuming the psychiatrist knew or should have known that his patient posed a risk of serious bodily harm and a specific target could be identified. Numerous other cases have since followed suit (See, e.g., *Bardoni v. Kim* (Mich. App.1986), although not all jurisdictions are uniform in their approach to these cases, nor do all reach a similar result.

Not all situations in which the obligations of a provider affect third persons (not a party to the physician-patient relationship) result in liability of the provider. For example, in *Chatman v. Millis* (Ark.1975), a divorced woman sought the services of a psychologist to determine whether her son's father might be sexually abusing him. After examining the child, the psychologist concluded that there was a likelihood of such abuse, and provided a report to that effect that was subsequently used in court. The psychologist, who was thereafter sued by the boy's father for an allegedly negligent diagnosis, defended on the basis that he had no physician-patient relationship with the father. The court agreed that no duty, and therefore no cause of action, existed on behalf of the father who was neither a patient nor a beneficiary of the professional who provided services.

One area that has seen voluminous litigation involving the rights of third parties is the employment context. Typically the issue is whether a physician who is engaged by an employer to perform an examination of an employee incurs a duty to the examinee to perform non-negligently. Usually one of two circumstances result from an allegedly negligent examination: either the patient is denied initial or continued employment, or the physician fails to diagnose a significant condition that might have been treated had it been discovered. Related cases have occurred in other contexts, such as when a physician employed by a life insurance company negligently examines an applicant, and insurance coverage is denied as a result.

The case of *Green v. Walker* (5th Cir.1990), is an example of the employment context. The plaintiff was required to submit to an annual physical examination as a condition of employment. The defendant physician engaged to perform the exam reported that all tests were normal and gave the highest possible rating. When the plaintiff was diagnosed with lung cancer one year later, he sued the physician claiming that the physician failed to discover his condition. The defendant's motion for summary judgment was granted on the basis that the physician, who was engaged by the employer, had no physician-patient relationship with the plaintiff and thus owed no duty of care to him. The federal court of appeals, sitting in a diversity case, reversed, holding that where an employee is required as a condition of employment to submit to examination, a physician-patient relationship is established. This relationship results in an obligation of due care, at least to the extent of the examination. This duty includes the obligation to make a reasonable and timely effort to communicate to the examinee any findings that pose an imminent threat to his or her well-being.

A variation on the theme, leading to a contrary result, occurred in *Keene v. Wiggins* (Cal.App.1977). In that case, an employee received worker's compensation benefits as a result of an injury sustained on the job. The employer engaged the defendant physician to review the matter, indicating his prognosis, including permanent disability. The physician diagnosed the plaintiff's condition as not amenable to further treatment, which diagnosis the plaintiff claimed that he relied upon. In a lawsuit that followed, the physician defended on the basis that no physician-patient relationship existed, and thus any duty extended only to the employer. The court agreed that in the absence of any special circumstances, it would be unusual for a claimant to rely on the report of a physician engaged by an adverse party. Thus the requirement that the claimant be examined does not necessarily establish a physician-patient relationship with an adverse party's agent, and no express or implied duty necessarily arises.

III.   THE LIMITS OF DUTY

Like most other agreements, those between physician and patient that result in the delivery of medical care can also be ended. Often they end in due course when the treatment is completed or when the patient dies or moves away from the area. Sometimes the physician-patient relationship ends when either the patient, or often both parties, agree that another physician will take over treatment of the patient. Sometimes the professional relationship ends because the physician determines that he no longer wants to treat the patient. This can occur for a number of reasons, including failure to pay for services, failure to show up for appointments, refusal to follow the treatment plan, and the physician's change of practice. The general rule is that a physician is entitled to terminate the professional relationship only after he has given the patient reasonable notice and opportunity to secure the services of another competent physician. The reasonableness of the opportunity to make alternate provisions depends upon the length of time given, the willingness of the physician to assist in locating a new practitioner, and the information provided to the patient which informs him about the status of his medical needs and the future course of treatment.

A. VOLUNTARY TERMINATION

In the event that a patient requires emergent care before actual termination, or an acute problem requires treatment before a referral is completed, the attending physician will likely owe a duty of continuing care until the condition stabilizes. Furthermore, a practitioner who terminates a patient and makes a referral might still be held liable for foreseeable complications if the referral is not made to a suitable practitioner. In *Longman v. Jasiek* (Ill.App.1980), for example, a dentist specializing in oral surgery operated on a patient prior to terminating her as a patient. When she thereafter developed complications, the dentist referred her to her family physician. The family physician was not successful in treating a post-operative infection, and the patient ultimately sued the dentist for failing to provide post-operative care or make a suitable referral to an oral surgeon. The dentist was ultimately held liable for the post-operative complications which likely would have been avoided if a proper referral was completed. Thus *Longman* demonstrates that a mere referral may not be adequate to defend against a charge of abandonment; the subsequent practitioner must also be suitable to meet the patient's needs. Furthermore, the referring physician may be liable not only for failing to inform the patient that a particular type of specialist is desirable, but also for a delay in obtaining subsequent care if a proper referral is not secured immediately.

The question of whether there are some circumstances in which a physician is precluded from terminating care of a patient is a difficult one. Under most circumstances, a physician who makes a proper referral offering suitable time and guidance is likely to avoid a later claim that he abandoned his patient. But what about a physician who expressly or implicitly agrees to render a particular course of treatment and wants to terminate the relationship before the services are completed? And what about a physician who agrees to perform a certain procedure but thereafter changes his mind and cannot find a subsequent practitioner? If a court ultimately finds that a contract was breached, an action may lie for damages consequent to the breach. This might include the time and expenses of pre-operative care (diagnostic tests, lab and x-ray costs, etc.) as well as any injury or deterioration in condition that the patient suffered as a result of the breach.

Causes of action for improper termination generally allege the tort of abandonment. A patient may be said to be abandoned when a physician interrupts a course of necessary treatment without proper notice and referral to a subsequent practitioner. This is sometimes referred to as an intentional abandonment. It should be distinguished from a negligent abandonment, which may be alleged when a physician, in the course of treatment, fails to attend to a patient as would reasonably be required under the circumstances. If, for example, a patient is prematurely discharged (see, e.g., *Wickline v. State* (Cal.App.1986)), this may give rise to a negligence action for abandonment and will be discussed further in Chapter 2, infra. Setting aside the confusion in terminology, the practical distinction is an evidentiary one: negligence actions generally require expert testimony as to the reasonable standard of care whereas intentional torts may be established on the basis of the deliberateness of the defendant's conduct.

In some situations, interruptions in the physician-patient relationship occur under circumstances that may be thought to excuse any neglect or conscious abandonment of the patient. For example, if the physician becomes ill or incapacitated himself, he may be temporarily or permanently unable to treat his patients. He also may or may not be able to provide reasonable notice or arrange alternative care. Generally, no liability results when a physician terminates treatment due to his own incapacity.

Another circumstance arises when physicians are unavailable when called upon due to prior emergencies, vacations, professional engagements or merely because they are not "on-call" when the need for their services exists. The law recognizes that medical necessities occur around the clock and no physician is expected to be available whenever the need arises. The obligation is to provide "reasonable" substitute care and to make patients aware of the exigencies that may require their care to be handled by another practitioner. For example, a rotation schedule of on-call physicians is a common practice to cover emergency patients or others who routinely require services at unpredictable times (e.g., expectant mothers). Except in those cases in which a physician specifically agrees to attend to a particular medical procedure, the use of substitute or on-call physicians is generally acceptable. Even then, if the physician is unavailable due to a prior emergency, abandonment should not occur. Of course, under such circumstances it is appropriate and necessary for the physician to explain the possible contingencies that might require another physician to attend to the patient.

Under circumstances where it is usual and customary for physicians to call upon their colleagues to substitute for them, some courts hold that specific notice need not be given to patients as long as the substitute physician is competent. See *Beatty v. Morgan* (Ga.App.1984). This is a minority view and the customary practice is to notify patients of the on-call system as well as the identity of those physicians who participate.

The need to select competent physicians to rotate on an on-call basis should be underscored. The general rule is that another physician is not liable for the professional misconduct of a physician who covers his practice (See *Settoon v. St. Paul Fire & Marine Ins. Co.* (La.App.1976)) (declining to hold one physician vicariously liable for the malpractice of another on-call physician). However, he may incur direct liability if he fails to select competent physicians with whom to share an on-call rotation. See infra, chapter 7. By the same token, a physician who relies upon others to substitute for him may also incur liability if he neglects to provide adequate instructions or flag the special needs of a patient. See *Reams v. Stutler* (Ky.1982).

Intentional abandonment of a patient can either be express or implied. In those cases in which a physician notifies his patients that he no longer intends to provide services but fails to provide a suitable alternative, or even allow enough time for the patient to do so, the abandonment is said to be express. See *Norton v. Hamilton* (Ga.App.1955) (physician withdrew from treatment of pregnant woman; patient delivered before she was allegedly able to find another physician). Abandonment is said to be implied if the physician acts in such a way as to deny treatment without expressly terminating the professional relationship. For example, if a patient appears for emergency care and a physician turns the patient away claiming that no treatment is needed, this might constitute an abandonment. Alternatively, if a physician refuses to provide a proper referral (including medical history) so that another physician can take over a patient's treatment, this may constitute an implied abandonment. See *Johnson v. Vaughn* (Ky.1963) (patient of one physician called upon another physician for emergency treatment; second physician called initial physician for release, but was not able to secure the necessary information in a suitable and timely fashion).

B.   REFUSAL TO PROVIDE TREATMENT

The question of whether a single physician, facility or group practice can decline to treat certain patients is a difficult one. In *Payton v. Weaver* (Cal.App.1982), a physician attempted to terminate his care of an end-stage renal patient who required kidney dialysis in order to maintain her life. The patient was reported to be intensely uncooperative, frequently missed or was late for appointments and refused to follow the physician's instructions for treatment, including getting treatment for her drug and alcohol dependency. The physician provided reasonable notice of termination, but the patient was unable to secure alternative treatment and thus petitioned the court for an order compelling further treatment. The parties entered a stipulation regarding treatment, which was subsequently violated by the patient. When the physician petitioned the court again for an order permitting termination, the court granted his request, even though no other dialysis unit was willing to take on the patient's care. The order of the trial court was affirmed on appeal, at least in part because there was evidence that the patient's participation in the program adversely affected other patients.

A contrary result, however, was reached in another California decision. In *Leach v. Drummond*

Medical Group, Inc. (Cal.App.1983), the plaintiffs were patients of a particular medical group. Dissatisfied with the performance of some of the physicians, the plaintiffs wrote to the state licensing board alleging a variety of complaints. When the group was notified of the allegations, it notified the plaintiffs of its intent to terminate their relationship on the basis that "a proper physician-patient relationship" could no longer be maintained. The plaintiffs sued, alleging a variety of causes of action, including one under the state civil rights act. After initially being denied relief by the trial court, the appellate court reversed. Finding that the complaint did state a claim upon which relief could be granted, the court held that while one physician may decline to treat a patient, an entire group (or hospital) did not necessarily have the same option. In that particular case, the group provided the only similar services available within approximately one hundred miles.

Finally, there are some circumstances under which a physician may have an ongoing obligation to former patients even after the termination of the physician-patient relationship. In a number of the *Dalkon Shield* cases, for example, physicians implanted the Dalkon Shield intrauterine device (IUD) in some patients with whom they later lost contact. When it became generally known within the profession that the Dalkon Shield had been linked to severe health risks, including sterility and even death, a number of courts held that the physicians incurred a duty to warn users of the potential hazards. A number of cases were brought upon physicians' failure to do so, some of which were successful. See *Tresemer v. Barke* (Cal.App.1978). Physicians, being in the best position to warn such patients, were generally obligated to make reasonable efforts to locate former patients and remove the device, if warranted.

Notwithstanding some of the foregoing exceptions, physician are generally not obligated to treat patients who they simply do not like. If a physician-patient relationship has already been initiated, proper notice of termination is necessary, along with whatever measures are reasonably necessary to secure treatment with another physician. The law does not require that a subsequent treating physician be in place. *Payton* demonstrates that termination can occur even if no other physician can be found to assume the patient's care. The standard is one of reasonableness, and an action for abandonment will not generally lie when sufficient grounds for termination exist, along with reasonable efforts on the part of the physician to find alternative care.

CHAPTER TWO

NEGLIGENCE–BASED CLAIMS

I. IN GENERAL: THE STANDARD
OF CARE

Negligence, the most common theory of liability in medical malpractice litigation, is defined as "conduct which falls below the standard established by law for the protection of others against unreasonable risk of harm." Restatement (Second) of Torts § 282 (1965). The negligence cause of action generally requires that four elements be established: (1) there exists an obligation of due care; (2) the duty is violated on the basis of the applicable standard of care; (3) whatever injuries or damages are sustained are proximately caused by the breach of duty; and (4) the plaintiff suffers compensable damages. The burden is on the plaintiff to establish each and every element of the negligence action.

The standard of conduct that is required to meet the obligation of "due care" is based upon what the "reasonable practitioner" would do in like circumstances. The standard is not one of excellence or superior practice; it only requires that the physician exercise that degree of skill and care that would be expected of the average qualified practitioner practicing under like circumstances. Such circumstances might include the location where the practitioner conducts his practice and even the school of medicine to which he adheres. Thus, in a particular case, if two or more alternative procedures might have been used and the defendant selected one, the issue is whether a competent physician would have done so, even if another would not. The standard is also not one of good faith; the fact that a physician meant well or practiced to the best of his ability is not relevant. Conduct is always measured by objective criteria in terms of how the reasonable practitioner would perform under like circumstances.

The use of objective criteria is not without its limits, however. Conduct involving professional skills and services is generally evaluated by standards determined by the profession; therefore what is objectively "right" does not always yield to consensus. Courts have not been entirely uniform in establishing the criteria that define a standard of care in any particular circumstance. Both courts and legislatures have, at various times, issued pronouncements about the standard of care for medical malpractice actions. For example, following the ruling of the Washington Supreme Court in *Helling v. Carey* (Wash.1974), in which the court specifically rejected evidence by uncontradicted testimony of the applicable professional standard, and instead imposed its own, the Washington legislature responded immediately. It enacted a law which declared that professional standards would henceforth be established by the profession and that courts were not free to reject such standards.

A. RESPECTABLE MINORITY RULE

One such limit of objective criteria concerns standards and procedures that are adopted on a day-to-day basis within the practice of medicine. Perhaps needless to say, in a profession as complicated as medicine, physicians often do not agree on the therapeutic approach that ought to be used in a particular case. Indeed, the entire concept of "second opinions" arose in recognition of different methods of approach to medical care. The fact that a practitioner chooses a particular method which ultimately yields a poor result does not lead to the conclusion that a poor method was chosen. In acknowledging that medical approaches to treatment do, in fact, vary and that courts are incapable of evaluating those kinds of judgments, most courts have adopted some sort of "respectable minority" test. In essence, the theory is that certain procedures which might not be adopted by a majority of practicing physicians might still be acceptable to a "respectable minority" of such practitioners. Thus, if a choice can be made among various alternative approaches to treating a particular condition and a respectable minority of physicians would have selected one such procedure, a physician will not be held liable for malpractice, assuming, of course, reasonable skill and care were exercised in providing such care.

In *Henderson v. Heyer–Schulte Corp.* (Tex.Civ. App.1980), however, a Texas court modified the standard to reflect what is doubtless a better approach to this matter. In *Henderson*, a physician performed a breast augmentation procedure which resulted in silicone leakage and movement throughout the patient's body. There was evidence that the particular technique had been used in the past by various qualified and respected members of the profession. The court held that the issue was not whether a "respectable minority" or "considerable number" of physicians practice a particular technique, but whether the procedure meets a minimal threshold of due care as determined by the "average qualified physician" standard.

B. SCHOOL AND LOCALITY RULES

The standard of care that is applicable to a particular physician has historically depended, at least in part, on where he (or she) practices and what "school" of treatment he follows. The so-called "school rule" is largely a historical reference to the days when there existed different recognized schools of treatment. For example, the homeopathic and allopathic schools differed in that latter, but not the former, uses agents that would cause different effects than those supposedly causing the disease. A practitioner from one school would not be expected to use a technique from another school. Contemporary examples include osteopathy and chiropractic (as distinct from medicine) and the theory remains that a practitioner from one school should only be held accountable according to the standards propounded by that school. For example, in some states osteopaths are not permitted to prescribe drugs or perform surgical procedures. In such cases, osteopaths would be held to the standard of care expected of osteopaths.

Even where they continue to exist, there are limits to the school rules. If, for instance, a patient voluntarily seeks the services of a chiropractor rather than orthopedist to treat a back problem, the patient may be reasonably expected to know that certain procedures (such as surgical intervention) will not be used. On the other hand, in *Mostrom v. Pettibon* (Wash.App.1980), a chiropractor was held liable for failing to identify and disclose that the patient had medical problems for which chiropractic treatment was inappropriate. Indeed, for all intents and purposes, the practical significance of school rules has largely been lost today as most practitioners are now held to the general standards of the medical profession.

As an adjunct to the school rule, physicians have also been held liable for their failure to recognize that a particular treatment issue was beyond their competence and should have been referred to a specialist for consultation and/or management. In *Pittman v. Gilmore* (5th Cir.1977), a general practitioner attempted to treat a patient who for two days was reportedly coughing up blood. The physician failed to appreciate the seriousness of the condition and did not refer the patient to a thoracic surgeon who might have been able to save the patient's life. The court held the general practitioner liable in negligence for failing to call in a specialist.

The standard of care expected of general practitioners and of specialists is another fertile area of litigation. In the typical case, a general practitioner who practices within that area of expertise and refers patients to specialists when unable to manage a particular patient (assuming that a specialist is available to the patient) will only be held to the standard of care of a generalist. A specialist, however, who holds himself out or represents that he is a specialist is generally held to a higher standard of care. See *Shilkret v. Annapolis Emergency Hospital Ass'n* (Md.1975) (stating that "... it has been generally accepted that where a physician holds himself out as a specialist, he is held to a higher standard of knowledge and skill than a general practitioner.") In fact, even in those cases in which a practitioner is not a specialist, but undertakes to perform services generally provided or even perhaps generally requiring the services of a specialist, such practitioner may also be held to the higher standard of care.

A related area involves practitioners who provide services in the allied health professions such as nursing, psychology and other fields. The standard of care generally expected of these professionals is that which would be expected of the average qualified practitioner practicing in that field. Once again, if the practitioner holds himself out as possessing greater knowledge or expertise, he is likely to be held to the higher standard. In *Simpson v. Davis* (Kan.1976), a general dentist who performed endodontic work on a patient was held to the standard of a specialist since that type of work was generally undertaken by specialists.

The geographical location where a physician practices has historically had a bearing on the standard of care to which he is held. The "locality rule" was justified in two ways. First, physicians practicing in rural locations had less opportunity to become educated and trained in new procedures and equipment, as well as less access to modern facilities. As a consequence, it would be unfair to hold them to the same standard of care as that of their urban colleagues, who had much greater opportunity for continuing medical education and access to new information and facilities. Secondly, in order to attract physicians to rural areas, which offer fewer incentives for practice (i.e., less opportunity for interactions with colleagues that lead to familiarity with the most up-to-date procedures, less modern equipment, and even access to patients and insurance) the protection of the locality rule was thought to create an incentive for physicians to practice in such communities. Specialization, in particular, is difficult in rural areas since the lesser patient volume makes it more difficult to support a practice.

The locality rule served primarily as a rule that would limit who could testify as an expert in a medical malpractice case. A physician outside of the same or similar locality would be precluded from testifying because he was thought not to have adequate knowledge of the relevant medical standard for a particular community. This was the "strict locality rule" and today it prevails only in a few jurisdictions.

In recent years courts have moved away from the kinds of geographical considerations that led to development of the locality rule. Recognizing that today's technology (including transportation and communication of information) makes it substantially easier for physicians in all locations to acquire the most up-to-date information and training, most states have moved away from locality considerations, instead adopting a more national standard of care. As to the subsidy justification which suggests that locality considerations are important in attracting physicians to rural locations, courts have noted that the locality rule often works an injustice. It is increasingly difficult in rural areas to get any physicians to testify at all, leading to the so-called "conspiracy of silence" which substantially limits the available pool of experts.

Today the geographic location of a malpractice defendant's practice is usually one factor to be considered by the jury, and it may even have a bearing on the weight given to the testimony of an expert outside of the locality. However, it has less impact than it did half a century ago, and it usually does not preclude an expert from testifying as to the relevant community standard. The waning of the locality rule does not ignore the fact that regional variations in practice do exist or that the latest technology available in an urban area may not be available in a rural one. Thus in most states today courts will hold that the applicable standard of care is that based upon practice in the "same or similar" location, with due regard for the state of medical science and the availability of certain knowledge and procedures at the time of the alleged malpractice. See, e.g., *Hall v. Hilbun* (Miss.1985); *Wall v. Stout* (N.C.1984).

Those jurisdictions which retain some form of the locality rule defend it in a number of ways. Some argue that notwithstanding the advances in communication and travel, certain communities still have less access to state-of-the-art techniques and equipment. Others argue that the combination of both less specialized equipment and the absence of local specialists instructing on the use of new procedures makes it difficult for rural practitioners to really keep abreast of their urban counterparts. Furthermore, since actual parity is so difficult, it has been argued that the lesser standard is necessary to encourage practitioners to enter a practice in rural locations distant from large medical centers.

The greatest concern today about using geographic frames of reference is the absence of standards to designate what constitutes a similar community for purposes of applying the locality rule. In general, a locality is similar to the one in question if it contains comparable medical facilities and practitioners have similar access to new knowledge about techniques and procedures. Since it is reasonable to allow the trier of fact to consider the nature of the facilities and equipment, as well as the availability of special equipment and more experienced physicians when necessary, the question of when a locality is similar to another becomes an important factor. In *Shilkret v. Annapolis Emergency Hospital Ass'n* (Md.1975), the court essentially rejected the locality rule, noting that some courts look to geographic proximity while others consider demographic factors such as population, size and economic factors such per capita income. Others, however, focus on medical factors such as the availability of research and laboratory facilities, teaching hospitals and modern equipment.

As a consequence of the concerns about the validity of locality rules, as well as the difficulties in application, many jurisdictions have either rejected the rule altogether or have subjected it to various limitations. For example, some courts have refused to apply geographic limitations on the standard of care that applies to specialists, instead requiring them to adhere to a standard applicable to specialists in general, and thus to keep abreast of national developments through whatever means are available to them. See, e.g., *Taylor v. Hill* (Me.1983).

A number of courts have rejected the locality rule altogether or have limited it to merely one factor for the trier of fact to consider. See *Shilkret v. Annapolis Emergency Hospital Ass'n*, supra, in which the court specifically held that the standard should include "advances in the profession, availability of facilities, specialization or general practice, proximity of specialists and special facilities, together with all other relevant considerations . . . ." The trend is clearly away from locality considerations, although they may continue to be asserted for some time. Even those courts which presently reject them are more likely to allow evidence of geographical considerations, but to give little weight to professional standards that are arguably different than a national standard.

C. BEST JUDGMENT RULE

The question of whether in some cases the obligation of a physician is to adhere not only to the standard of the "average qualified practitioner" but to some higher standard is a difficult one. If, in a certain situation, a physician believes the acceptable medical practice to be unreasonably dangerous and he has sufficient expertise to know of a better practice, does he have an obligation to use his superior knowledge and skill? If so, can he be held accountable if he fails to do so? (Of course, if the practitioner adheres to a standard of care that is inferior to that of the average qualified practitioner, he is not shielded from liability on the basis that he exercised his best judgment.)

There is case law to support the proposition that a practitioner with superior skill or knowledge has a duty to exercise a higher standard, making him accountable in negligence if he fails to do so. The principle was first articulated in *Toth v. Community Hospital at Glen Cove* (N.Y.1968). In that case a pediatrician faced with dangerously ill premature twins recommended a course of action that was intended to keep them alive and prevent brain damage. Although there was evidence that this constituted accepted medical practice at the time, there was also evidence that a new study showed that such treatment was of little value and imposed an unnecessary risk of irreversible eye damage, which did, in fact, occur. The court held that "evidence that the defendant followed customary practice is not the sole test of professional malpractice" and noted that "if a physician fails to employ his expertise or best judgment ... he should not automatically be freed from liability because he adhered to acceptable practice." Rather, "a physician would use his best judgment and whatever superior knowledge, skill and intelligence he has."

In a subsequent New York case testing nearly the same issue, a pediatric resident prescribed a certain level of oxygen for a premature infant which was consistent with good medical care. His order was countermanded, however, by a pediatric instructor who was allegedly studying the effects of increased oxygen on such babies. In fact, the baby had been doing well on the conventional treatment, but the study called for the conventional treatment on one out of every three infants, and increased the oxygen for two of the three. The increased oxygen ultimately proved dangerous, and a lawsuit against the instructor followed. In finding liability on behalf of the instructor, the court stated:

Without in any way challenging the legitimacy of the debate ... as to the effect of the curtailment of oxygen on premature infants, we find it difficult to believe that any reputable institution would permit two out of three patients to receive unusual treatment, which might result in death or brain damage, unless it was fairly convinced that the conventional wisdom no longer applied.... Dr. Engle and the hospital cannot avail themselves of the shield of acceptable medical practice....

Burton v. Brooklyn Doctors Hospital (N.Y.A.D. 1982). The difficulty in applying the "best judgment rule" arises in those cases in which a practice potentially better than the industry standard also imposes some risks. If one of the risks materializes, the physician may expose himself to liability for not following the professional standard. The only real answer is that there exist a number of protections based upon such principles as the "respectable minority" rule and the "error in judgment" rule that assist a practitioner exercising his best judgment in being adequately protected. Nevertheless, there is still the potential for conflicting obligations between standards of practice and legal liability. This is especially true if a practitioner limits his best judgment to practice and procedures that do not incur added risk.

II. PROVING THE PROFESSIONAL STANDARD

The vast majority of medical malpractice cases require proof of negligence which is secured through expert testimony. Since it is usually difficult, if not virtually impossible, for lay jurors to assess the appropriate standard of care (and whether or not it has been violated the assistance of expert testimony is critical. With the burden of proof and persuasion resting with the plaintiff, the plaintiff must usually offer the testimony of an expert or risk a directed verdict for the defendant.

The difficulty that a plaintiff faces in securing expert testimony should not be understated. A so-called "conspiracy of silence" that is thought to exist among practitioners, particularly those in small, rural locations refers to their reluctance in malpractice actions to testify against one another. This "conspiracy" is thought to exist for a number of reasons, including the fear that the colleague may retaliate, particularly if the next time the "expert" becomes a defendant. Furthermore, there is the concern that physicians who become involved in legal matters may not get referrals from other colleagues or even insurers. By far, however, the greatest justification for the "conspiracy of silence" is that physicians often feel that it is morally objectionable, perhaps disloyal, to testify against "one's own". In some cases the remedy for experts being unavailable to plaintiffs is the use of so-called "hired guns". These are physicians who make a practice of getting involved in litigation, including testifying, and move from one case to another performing as an expert witness. Often they attempt to testify in a variety of cases, even without a genuine expertise in a particular field. In recent years the standards concerning qualification of expert witnesses have made it more difficult for "hired guns" to participate in cases for which they have little expertise.

In contrast to the difficulties often experienced by malpractice plaintiffs in finding suitable and willing expert witnesses, defendants are generally much more successful in finding agreeable colleagues who will come to their defense. Physicians asked to participate in litigation on behalf of defendants may still be reluctant, but generally they object to the time-consuming nature of the practice (particularly being available for trial at unpredictable times) as well as have an overall dislike of the litigation process. Today many courts have addressed the burdensome nature of the legal process by allowing such things as videotaped expert testimony when appropriate. In any event, defendants generally are able to find suitable expert testimony without significant difficulty.

A. COMPETENCY OF EXPERTS

Practitioners who are called upon to serve as expert witnesses are generally required to be knowledgeable (and preferably experienced) in the appropriate standard of care in a particular matter. To be knowledgeable includes both locality considerations (if the jurisdiction adheres to any form of locality rule) and general knowledge about the standard of care to be applied under the circumstances. This does not mean that the witness must necessarily be of the same specialty as the defendant or that he even necessarily follow the same school of medicine. For example, in *Bartimus v. Paxton Community Hospital* (Ill.App.1983), the court was willing to qualify a physician to testify against an osteopath, assuming that he could demonstrate sufficient familiarity with the standards of osteopathy.

With respect to specialists, courts are generally willing to find that a specialist is capable of testifying as to the standard of care expected of a general practitioner. The reverse, on the other hand, is not necessarily true: a general practitioner may or may not be qualified to testify against a specialist, even if he claims to be familiar with the applicable standards. See *Taylor v. Hill* (Me.1983) (permitting the testimony). Some courts, however, have held that general practitioners are *per se* disqualified to testify against specialists, regardless of their demonstrated familiarity with the necessary standard of care. What is typically required is that the court be satisfied that the purported expert is familiar with the applicable standard of care and that he is able to determine whether there is a causal connection between a violation of that standard and the injuries that are presented.

The testimonial competence of witnesses offered as experts is a matter that is handled in two alternative ways by the trial courts. Most seem to hold that in order for an expert to testify and offer an expert opinion, he must first establish that he meets a minimum threshold of competence. Thus the first part of an expert's testimony will establish his credentials and any other matters that bear upon his ability to offer an "expert" opinion. Many courts, after taking evidence on that issue (and cross-examination, if necessary) will provisionally "qualify" the expert to testify, or decline to do so, in which case he would not be permitted to testify further. The court's determination about the threshold qualification of experts is determined by applicable statute or case law.

The alternative to requiring a threshold inquiry about whether a particular expert is qualified to testify is to wait and see what exactly he is asked to comment upon. On that basis a court will thereafter determine whether he is qualified to do so. The determination about whether an expert is competent is one generally made by the court, whereas the weight that will be accorded to that testimony is generally a matter for the jury. In a few jurisdictions, there are statutory requirements concerning the qualification of expert witnesses.

The determination of whether a witness offered as an expert is competent to testify is generally made on the basis of two factors: whether he is familiar with the course of treatment in question (including its purpose, contraindications, risks and alternatives) and whether he is familiar with the relevant professional standard at the time the procedure was adopted. This determination is made after the plaintiff lays a foundation for the expert testimony, and has an opportunity to demonstrate that a proposed expert witness has sufficient expertise to qualify as an expert. Evaluating these factors is exclusively within the discretion of the trial judge.

The fact that an expert claims to have the necessary familiarity is not conclusive. In *Gilmore v. O'Sullivan* (Mich.App.1981), a proposed expert in obstetrics and gynecology was not permitted to testify as an expert in a case involving prenatal care and delivery of an infant. Finding that the "expert" was not board-certified in obstetrics and gynecology and that there was insufficient evidence of practical and research experience, the court refused to qualify him as an expert witness. While occupational experience used to be a traditional requirement, (see *Reinhardt v. Colton* (Minn.1983)), the trend today is toward more flexibility in what constitutes familiarity with professional standards. Thus, a physician who has the necessary experience in the general field and sufficient basic training may still qualify.

B. EXCEPTIONS TO THE NEED FOR EXPERT TESTIMONY

The difficulty that plaintiffs experience in locating competent experts to testify on their behalf is only one reason that expert testimony is sometimes impractical. Another is the expense involved. Physicians often charge a premium (on their already exorbitant fees) for their willingness to serve as an expert witness. In order to render an opinion, the expert must acquire substantial familiarity with the plaintiff's case and surrounding circumstances. Usually he must issue a report. Often he will submit to a deposition. All of this is required even before trial. Insurance, of course, does not pay for litigation. And even if a case is being handled on a contingency basis, the expert costs accrue and often must be paid up front, regardless of whether there is a favorable outcome. In fact, many meritorious cases are never pursued merely because of the prohibitive cost of expert witnesses. As a result, great attention has been paid in recent years to finding ways of pursuing a medical malpractice case without the need for expert testimony.

1. Defendant's Own Testimony

Unlike criminal defendants who can assert the "Fifth Amendment", thus invoking their privilege not to testify against themselves, civil defendants have no comparable right. There is nothing that prevents the plaintiff from calling the defendant physician on behalf of the plaintiff and requiring that he testify to facts that are within his own knowledge. Here he acts as a "percipient" or "fact" witness and whatever testimony that the plaintiff can elicit from him is valid and usable. The question of whether, additionally, he must also be willing to provide expert testimony is a more difficult one. The old rule was usually that a defendant not be so required because to do so would be unfair. In recent years, however, courts, sensitive to the difficulties of plaintiffs in securing medical experts, have been more willing to allow enough inquiry of the defendant to establish the requisite standard of care. In *McDermott v. Manhattan Eye, Ear and Throat Hospital* (N.Y.1964), the appellate court reversed the trial court's exclusion of the plaintiff's questioning of the defendant physician as to the applicable standard of care in his field on the basis of a textbook that he had written on the subject. Recognizing the difficulty in providing expert testimony, the court noted that "the plaintiff's only recourse in many cases may be to question the defendant doctor . . . in the hope that he will thereby be able to establish his malpractice claim. There is nothing unfair about such a practice."

Assuming that the defendant can be required to testify as an expert in his own case, the value of such testimony is still a critical issue. Obviously there is no guarantee that his expert "opinion" will be consistent with proving the plaintiff's case. More likely, he will make every effort to sabotage it. Even if books and treatises are introduced, doubtless he will attempt to minimize their value or their relevance to the case. As a result, it is clearly better strategy to have other means of establishing the essential elements of the plaintiff's case and to rely on testimony or admissions of the defendant to the least extent possible.

A significant testimonial matter arises when a defendant is called as an expert witness. An expert witness is not initially an adverse (or "hostile") one, and the rule that generally allows adverse witnesses to be interrogated through leading questions and impeached by their own testimony is not necessarily applicable. The modern trend, however, is to recognize an opposing party as an adverse witness and allow him to be examined as such.

Yet another difficult matter is determining whether a physician's out-of-court statements that are admissible as exceptions to the hearsay rule may be used in lieu of expert testimony. In *Wickoff v. James* (Cal.App.1958), the plaintiff's husband overheard the defendant admit to another physician, "Boy, I made a mess of things." Furthermore, he admitted to the husband that he had severed the patient's intestine while inserting a sigmoidoscope into the rectum. The court held that these statements constituted declarations against interest and that they were sufficient to serve in lieu of expert testimony.

2. Common Knowledge

A second potential means of avoiding the expert testimony requirement is through use of the "common knowledge" doctrine. This is available when the practitioner's negligence occurs in a manner that is so evident to a lay jury that the need for expert testimony is obviated. Thus if the fact finder can call upon his own knowledge and wisdom and apply a suitable standard of care without the aid of expert testimony, the plaintiff may be entitled to a ruling that expert testimony is not required. For example, a patient who undergoes a mastectomy on the wrong breast does not require the testimony of an expert to persuade the jury that the action constitutes malpractice. In *Killingsworth v. Poon* (Ga.App.1983), the common knowledge doctrine was invoked to demonstrate that the defendant who injected the patient in the shoulder was liable in negligence for a resulting puncture to the patient's lung.

The current trend in malpractice cases, at least among some courts, has been to expand the scope of cases in which common knowledge allows a case to overcome a directed verdict and make it to the jury. For example, in *Pry v. Jones* (Ark.1972), the court allowed common knowledge to let a case go to the jury in which it was alleged that the plaintiff's ureter was severed while she underwent a hysterectomy. Although there was also evidence that the procedure was complicated and by its nature it required an incision in close proximity to the ureter, the case was nevertheless permitted to go to the jury with "common knowledge" in lieu of expert testimony.

Other cases, however, have not been so generous. In *Ward v. Levy & Unger* (Mass.App.1989), the plaintiff allegedly suffered a facial injury during a tooth extraction. An offer of proof was made consisting only of the patient's own affidavit, medical records and photographs and a letter from the surgeon treating the facial injury. No evidence was offered on the causal connection between the alleged negligence and the injury. The court held that common knowledge was not sufficient to establish that link and that a jury would be left to conjecture without expert testimony. This case seems to demonstrate the inherent difficulty in small cases: a laceration on the face may have occurred on the basis of the defendant's negligence; however, the small extent of damages will probably not warrant the expenses of a medical expert.

Yet another recent case demonstrates that common knowledge is only reserved for cases in which it would be obvious to a lay jury that an injury resulted from professional negligence. In *Evanston Hospital v. Crane* (Ill.App.1993), the plaintiff, who failed to submit an expert affidavit in a summary judgment proceeding, claimed that he should have been referred to a cardiologist because he was diagnosed with a heart condition. He further contended that it was in the common knowledge of a lay person to make such a judgment. The court rejected his claim, holding that whether a patient should be referred to a specialist is not properly resolved by the common knowledge of a lay person.

3. Violation of a Statute

When a defendant violates a civil or criminal statute, ordinance or regulation and the plaintiff claims that the violation is causally related to his injuries, such violation might support an allegation of negligence, even without expert testimony. In these cases, two issues must be resolved. The first is whether the statute or regulation is intended both to protect persons such as the plaintiff and to prevent the type of injury that the plaintiff allegedly sustained. Without a sufficient causal connection, the mere fact that a regulation was violated does not obviate the need for expert testimony. Secondly, it must be determined what procedural effect the violation should be given. In an appropriate case, the violation of the statute is considered to be "negligence *per se* " or "statutory negligence" and expert testimony may not be required to establish negligence.

Landeros v. Flood (Cal.1976) illustrates this principle. In that case an 11–month old baby was brought to the emergency room suffering from an injury that seemed to have been inflicted by a twisting action. No explanation was given for the injury. The physician failed to diagnose battered child syndrome, and also failed to do an x-ray on the child's head, which would have revealed a skull fracture. The child was discharged to his mother's home, where he was severely injured again. The purpose of an existing statute which requires mandatory reporting of child abuse is to protect children at risk from further injury. A resulting lawsuit was permitted on the basis that the physician breached his statutory duty to report the child's injuries, and that further injury ensued.

Violation of a statute can be alleged in the plaintiff's case, even if it does not obviate the need for expert testimony. In such a case, the procedural effect will likely not be that an expert needs to testify, but the violation may bear upon the standard of care and be introduced as part of the plaintiff's prima facie case.

Assuming that violation of a statute is found, it is not necessarily true that the violation conclusively establishes negligence. Some courts seem to hold that such a violation establishes a rebuttable presumption of negligence. In those cases the plaintiff is not initially entitled to a directed verdict, but may later get one if the defendant is not able to rebut the presumption of negligence. A seeming majority of courts hold that violations of a statute result in evidence of negligence, noting that it is up to the jury to determine what weight the evidence should be given.

An example of those cases in which violation of a statute is not necessarily probative of negligence is when it is a licensing statute that is allegedly violated. If a practitioner is found to be practicing without a license and commits an act of alleged negligence, is the absence of a license probative on the issue of whether the act was negligent? The answer seems to depend upon whether the absence of a license was due to a determination on the part of the licensing authority that the practitioner was not fit to practice or whether it amounted to some sort of oversight. A Massachusetts court so held in *McCarthy v. Boston City Hospital* (Mass.1971). In that case the physician's absence of a license seemed to occur as a result of a lapse in his registration. It did not appear, however, that it in any way affected the quality of his patient care. The court held that the absence of a license did not constitute a proximate cause of the patient's injury.

In those cases in which the absence of a license results because the license was revoked, suspended or never obtained, it is more likely to be probative on the issue of competence to practice, whether or not an actual causal connection is found.   In *Stahlin v. Hilton Hotels Corp.* (7th Cir.1973), violation of a statute was held to be probative when a nurse who violated the Nursing Act by practicing without a license was found to not have the qualifications required of nurses and thus was not competent to perform the services that led to the claim of malpractice.

4. Medical Literature and Manufacturers' Instructions

The question of whether medical literature might be used in lieu of a medical expert depends, initially, upon whether the literature is even admissible and thereafter, upon what probative value it will be given.   The general rule is that most literature is not admissible to prove the truth of what it contains because it constitutes hearsay.   *See generally,* 84 A.L.R.2d 1338 (1962, Supp.1979, 1984).   There is an exception, however, recognized by the Federal Rules of Evidence (see Fed. R. Evid. Rule 803 (18)) and by a growing number of states (see West's Mass. Gen. Laws Ann. ch. 233, § 79C [Supp.1985]). The exception recognizes medical literature, including treatises, as reliable authority within the profession.   Such literature can either be introduced on direct examination of an expert who relies on it or is asked to comment upon it in his testimony, or it can be introduced during cross-examination of an expert who is asked to comment upon its reliability as well as its content.

The objection to use of medical literature, particularly in lieu of experts, is the lack of opportunity for cross-examination. The author of such a text does not appear in court; therefore, he or she cannot be cross-examined. Nor can the text be examined as to how individual variations that exist in actual cases affect the conclusions in the treatise. Furthermore, the effect of treatises on a lay jury is uncertain. Some jurors are unable to understand them and as a consequence tend to discount the evidence. Others do just the opposite, giving undue deference merely because it appears as published literature. Furthermore, because many medical techniques and procedures are time-sensitive, it is not always possible to determine what the standard of practice was at a given time. A particular passage may be written two to three years before the date of publication.

There is also the problem that different medical literature may be favorable to different parties' cases. What happens if there is contrary literature introduced? Credibility is usually determined on the basis of observation of demeanor of the person testifying. Juries have little ability to assess the credibility of conflicting treatises or to understand the reasons for differing opinions on a particular subject. In these cases medical literature is generally not relied upon in lieu of an expert, but is only used to bolster the credibility of an expert who is able to present the treatise and testify about its reliability and relevance to the case.

The question arises as to whether medical literature, in and of itself, is probative enough for establishing a medical fact that it is sufficient to get to the jury. The answer seems to be that it would be difficult to offer the treatise into evidence without a medical "expert" to comment upon its validity in a particular case. When the purpose of the literature is to obviate the need for an expert, the "expert" called upon is generally the defendant himself. Thus if it appears that there is a treatise on point, and that the defendant will establish the relevance and reliability of the treatise, the final hurdle is to establish on the basis of any admissions in prior testimony (e.g., by deposition) that the testimony, along with the treatise, is sufficient to get to the jury.

Information provided by product manufacturers is handled differently. The type of information that may be contained in a package insert of a drug, for example, contains warnings, side effects, contraindications for use, etc. The Food and Drug Administration (FDA) requires that all drugs, unless otherwise exempt, be approved for patient use. It also requires that prescription drugs be packaged with an informational insert that describes the drug and gives a detailed explanation of its use. Other items prepared with manufacturer's instructions have been the subject of malpractice litigation, particularly on the issue of how the manufacturer's information affects the standard of care.

In those jurisdictions which recognize an exception to the hearsay rule for medical literature, including treatises, generally the same exception applies since nearly the same material contained in the package insert is reiterated in the Physicians' Desk Reference (PDR), a publication, updated annually, that contains extensive information about drug products and is generally considered to be a reliable source. Even in those jurisdictions that do not recognize a hearsay exception, it has been argued that the package insert is not hearsay, particularly if offered for a reason other than the truth of information contained within it. For example, if the issue is whether the physician should have been on notice of a contraindication in the use of a particular product, the package insert may be probative on that issue.

Medical literature, treatises and package inserts are the typical type of evidence that experts will bring into court and rely upon in providing their testimony. Only on rare occasion might a court permit a research study to be admitted as evidence. In *Young v. Horton* (Mont.1993), the court admitted a number of journal articles in a case in which the plaintiff denied that she had given consent to surgery. The essence of the articles was that patients frequently forget when the consent involves a surgical procedure.

The question of whether manufacturers' literature such as a package insert, in and of itself, is sufficient to get to the jury is again a difficult one. Clearly in conjunction with a testifying expert, the insert, assuming admissibility, can provide valuable information. By the same token, if the defendant will provide the "expert" testimony, the package insert or other manufacturers' literature can assist in proving the plaintiff's case. Further, if the common knowledge doctrine is otherwise applicable, the manufacturer's literature in conjunction with common knowledge should generally suffice. Whether a manufacturer's literature without common knowledge is sufficient to get to the jury is still a difficult question. The case law is sparse and conflicting. In *Ohligschlager v. Proctor Community Hospital* (Ill.1973), the court suggested that the literature provided by the manufacturer might be adequate in a liability case against a physician to get beyond a directed verdict. However, in the subsequent case of *Mielke v. Condell Memorial Hospital* (Ill.App. 1984), the holding in *Ohligschlager* was limited to physicians. As to a standard of care expected of hospitals, manufacturers' literature alone was not sufficient to get the plaintiff to the jury.

The reasons that plaintiffs attempt to use manufacturers literature in lieu of medical experts is generally the same as for the use of the common knowledge doctrine: medical experts are difficult to obtain and either too expensive for cases that do not warrant expert fees or the plaintiff is simply unable to afford them. When the information contained in this literature is on point it becomes a valuable source of timely and accurate information. However, it is also important to ensure that the literature is relevant and material to the case, as well as understandable to a lay jury. This means that the literature must actually reflect the state of knowledge and practice in the profession, and not some ideal standard that is not actually practiced. The defendant, of course, is entitled to contradict the evidence and demonstrate that it is not consistent with the industry standard. That does not affect the literature's admissibility, however, unless it tends to deviate so far as to vitiate its probative value.

5. Res Ipsa Loquitur

Probably the largest exception to the requirement that plaintiffs bear the burden of proof in establishing liability is advanced in those cases in which there is little direct evidence of negligence, but there is significant indirect or circumstantial evidence. Known as "res ipsa loquitur" (or, literally, "the thing speaks for itself"), the res ipsa doctrine is invoked in cases where negligence can only be established by drawing an inference from the circumstances. Generally these circumstances include a mishap for which there is no credible explanation and which does not occur in the absence of someone being negligent.

The seminal case establishing the applicability of res ipsa loquitur was the 1863 English case of *Byrne v. Boadle* (1863). In that case the plaintiff, while walking down the street, was hit in the head with a barrel of flour which had fallen out of a warehouse window as he walked below. The warehouse was owned by the defendant. The court invoked the doctrine of res ipsa loquitur, holding that in the absence of negligence, barrels of flour do not generally fall out of windows.

The res ipsa doctrine is largely in tact today. In an applicable case, its effect is to shift the burden of proof to the defendant to explain why he was not negligent and, in the absence of a credible explanation, to permit (but not require) the jury to infer negligence. Some courts prefer to explain the effect of res ipsa loquitur as establishing the plaintiff's prima facie case of negligence, and thus the case goes to the jury on that basis.

The application of the doctrine to medical malpractice cases has not been without reservation. Often it is applied to those cases in which a mishap occurs while a patient is unconscious or otherwise unable to determine what or why there was a particular occurrence. It is not intended to make the physician an insurer of a particular result, nor is it intended to create liability on the part of the physicians merely because a bad outcome results. Res ipsa is thus not applicable when any known or perceived risk to a certain procedure occurs. It is reserved solely for those unexplained occurrences with generally do not happen unless there is negligence.

Application of the res ipsa loquitur doctrine generally requires that three conditions be present: the occurrence of a mishap which typically does not occur in the absence of someone being negligent; the instrumentality which apparently caused the accident must be within the exclusive control of the defendant; and it must appear that the plaintiff did not in any way contribute to his own injury. The availability of res ipsa loquitur for a particular fact situation is a matter for the discretion of the trial court, and the effect given to it by most courts is that a permissive inference of negligence is permitted. The permissive inference of negligence is not tantamount to a presumption, rebuttable or conclusive. The jury is free to accept or reject the inference, and thus no evidence on behalf of the defendant is required for a verdict for the defendant. The only clear procedural effect is that the case will go to the jury, and the plaintiff can rest, even without introducing expert testimony on the issue of causation, and still get to the jury.

The purpose behind the res ipsa doctrine is to assist patients who sustain some sort of injury or untoward consequence of a medical procedure for which it was impossible for them to know what might have happened to cause it. The most difficult part of sustaining the burden of demonstrating the applicability of res ipsa is showing that the mishap does not generally occur in absence of negligence. This is not an "expert" standard; it is something to be determined by the average person in light of ordinary experience and as a consequence of common knowledge. Among the most common situations in which res ipsa has been invoked are those cases alleging that a medical instrument or sponge was left inside a patient during surgery.

The application of res ipsa loquitur does not obviate the need to establish causation in a case to which it is invoked. It will likely assist in establishing fault by use of circumstantial evidence that is probative of causation, but the burden of proof on the causation issue still remains initially with the plaintiff. As a result, sometimes expert testimony is also used to help meet the elements of the res ipsa doctrine. For example, in *Hale v. Venuto* (Cal. App.1982) the plaintiff suffered peroneal and tibial palsy in her foot after undergoing surgery on her kneecap to correct a dislocation. The plaintiff produced expert testimony to the effect that the injury was probably a result of negligence. On appeal, the court allowed application of the res ipsa doctrine, even though there had been adequate expert testimony on the issue of causation. The court's conclusion was reached on the basis of all of the evidence, including the common knowledge doctrine.

The requirement that the defendant have exclusive control of the instrumentality that apparently caused the injury has been construed broadly by some courts, including the one in the landmark case of *Ybarra v. Spangard* (Cal.1944). In that case the plaintiff underwent an appendectomy, only to later experience sharp pain in his right shoulder. He subsequently suffered atrophy and eventually paralysis of the shoulder muscles. A lawsuit was brought against all of the defendants who were present during the procedure, including the anesthesiologist, the primary and consulting surgeons and a number of hospital employees. The owner of the hospital was also named. Of course, it was likely that at least some of the defendants were not negligent, but the purpose of the res ipsa doctrine is to infer that there was negligence by any or all of them, making it incumbent upon them to come forward and explain what happened. The hope is that if res ipsa is invoked against all of them, each will be encouraged to reveal what he/she knows. Without res ipsa, each defendant could sit back, engage in a conspiracy of silence, and insist that the plaintiff prove his own case.

The *Ybarra* court permitted use of res ipsa, even though it was clear that not all defendants even had actual control over the defendant. Rather, the court held that the test was a "right of control" and that under that standard each had the burden of explaining the cause of the defendant's injury. The court justified its departure from the traditional res ipsa limits by explaining that the special relationship between physician and patient requires that responsibility for the mishap be assumed by those to whom the patient entrusted his care.

The requirement that the plaintiff demonstrate that he did not, in any way, contribute to his own injury is generally the least difficult part of the plaintiff's burden. Often patients are anesthetized when the injury occurs; generally they have entrusted their care to the physician; and in any event patients usually do not act in ways that contribute to a result otherwise caused by medical malpractice. Patients do, of course, decline medical care; they elect among alternative procedures and sometimes they act against medical advice. In so doing, they can bring about a medical condition or exacerbate an existing one. They generally do not, however, voluntarily cause a mishap while under the exclusive care of a physician. Thus if the first conditions of res ipsa are met (an injury that ordinarily does not occur in the absence of negligence and exclusive control of the instrumentality with the defendant) the absence of contributory negligence usually occurs as well.

Res ipsa also has its limitations, both statutory and practical. Under North Dakota law, for example, the doctrine is not applicable in medical malpractice cases unless the breach is so egregious that it would amount to common knowledge that a layman would comprehend. Thus in *Maguire v. Taylor* (8th Cir.1991), for example, the doctrine was held not apply to a case involving nerve damage since it was beyond the basic understanding of lay jurors to determine whether it could happen in the absence of negligence.

Courts also differ on whether the court or the jury is to decide whether the basic elements of the res ipsa doctrine have been satisfied. Some courts hold that if the plaintiff's case meets a certain threshold (i.e., "reasonable minds can differ") the jury is left to determine whether the elements have been proved. See *Sammons v. Smith* (Iowa 1984). Others hold that the court is to determine whether the elements of res ipsa are satisfied and, if so, for the jury to evaluate all of the evidence and determine the procedural effect of applying the doctrine.

Assuming that it is determined that res ipsa is applicable, the usual consequence is that the case goes to the jury with the instruction that it is permitted but not required to infer that the plaintiff's injury resulted from negligence. Courts differ, however, on the effect of expert testimony that some plaintiffs also offer to support the inference of negligence. The traditional rule has been that if expert testimony is needed to bolster plaintiff's argument about negligence, it is not a proper case for res ipsa. Res ipsa is reserved for those cases in which the common knowledge of lay jurors was adequate to create the inference. See *Marquis v. Battersby* (Ind.App.1982). Unless the expert testimony was completely unnecessary, it removed the case from a "common knowledge" theme to one requiring the aid of expert testimony.

The current trend seems to be toward expanding the availability of res ipsa and allowing it to be applied both in "common knowledge" cases in which the inference can be made exclusively by the lay juror and in those cases where expert testimony is supplied to support the inference. See *Horner v. Northern Pac. Beneficial Ass'n Hosps., Inc.* (Wash. 1963). Under this view the purpose of the res ipsa doctrine is to yield a permissive inference of negligence in those cases where the elements can be established, by whatever means. Thus the use of expert testimony to support the common knowledge which would lead to an inference does not render the doctrine inapplicable. Res ipsa is not merely a facet of "common knowledge"; it is a separate doctrine with a theory and a purpose which is to allow the use of circumstantial evidence when the necessary prerequisites are met.

Not surprisingly, in a number of cases in which res ipsa would probably carry the day, plaintiffs have nevertheless been reluctant to rely upon it since if it is held inapplicable, the absence of a liability expert would likely be fatal to the case. As a result, it is common today to invoke res ipsa, but also to supply expert testimony to be certain that liability is established. Particularly in those jurisdictions where the presence of expert testimony does not render res ipsa inapplicable, it is common to plead in the alternative: specific acts of negligence as demonstrated by the expert testimony, and res ipsa as to those acts for which it is not clear how they may have occurred. See *Reilly v. Straub* (Iowa 1979). In other courts, however, the pleading of specific acts of negligence precludes resort to the res ipsa doctrine since the primary source of evidence will not be circumstantial.

Finally, a few courts have added an additional element to the prerequisites for invoking res ipsa. The additional element is that the defendant be in a better position than the plaintiff to determine the cause of plaintiff's injury. If, for example, the plaintiff was anesthetized when the injury occurred, this condition would likely be met. *Horner*, supra. If, however, an injury occurs under circumstances that it is not clear to anyone exactly what happened, application of the doctrine is more doubtful since it would likely take an expert to establish causation. In any event, it is difficult to imagine a case in which the basic res ipsa elements are met, but the defendant would not be in a better position to determine the cause of the injury.

The consequence of the permissive inference that res ipsa yields is to permit the jury to determine the overall credibility of the plaintiff's case, in light of the evidence, testimony and cross-examination of the witnesses. It does not require that the jury accept the permissive inference allowed by the doctrine; it also does not affect the credibility of the defendant's evidence or overall presentation. It also does not preclude the defendant from testifying that he conformed to the applicable standard of care, without offering an explanation for the plaintiff's injury. Without such an explanation, res ipsa does not necessarily mean that the plaintiff prevails. A defendant who testifies credibly that he did everything in his power to exercise due care, and the reason for the occurrence is unknown to him, the jury is entitled to come back with a defendant's verdict even if the res ipsa elements have been satisfied.

CHAPTER THREE

INTENTIONAL TORTS

I. IN GENERAL: HARM AND INTENT

As discussed in chapter 2, the predominant theory of liability in a medical malpractice action is negligence. Negligence connotes an unintended act that causes harm or, less commonly, an intended act that unintentionally causes harm. An alternative to negligence theory that is sometimes seen in medical malpractice litigation is intentional tort. In such actions the defendant is not necessarily alleged to have intentionally harmed the patient; rather, he intentionally acted in a fashion that ultimately caused harm to the patient. The practitioner's actions were not a consequence of mistake. Indeed, the practitioner expected the result that was achieved, but did not expect that the patient would later complain about his actions. Thus a medical procedure poorly performed might constitute negligence, while a medical procedure correctly performed that was not consented to might constitute an intentional tort.

Intentional torts strongly suggests that an element of "intent" accompanies the commission of the tort. Sometimes, however, the intent is inferred from the circumstances. For example, if informed consent is lacking, the elements of a battery may be established by inferring that there was an intention to act without consent. See infra at chapter 4. If intangible interests are affected (e.g., a right of privacy), the inference of intent may be satisfied by knowledge of the likely consequences of the action. Often intentional torts occur under conditions that the practitioner believes he has performed competently and rightly, only later to discover that his actions were tortious. Of course, in other situations, practitioners who commit intentional torts know of what they are doing, presumably believing that a lawsuit will not result.

The practical consequences of intentional torts are significant. First, the need for expert testimony generally required in a negligence action to establish the standard of care and the breach of that standard may be obviated. The critical element to prove is "intent" and expert testimony is usually not probative on that issue.

Secondly, a practitioner who is insured for his acts of negligence may find that his professional liability insurance policy disclaims coverage for intentional acts. A plaintiff often faces a serious dilemma when contemplating characterization of professional acts as intentional, thereby potentially cutting off the major source of payment of the claim.

Third, a claim may lie in intentional tort even if there is little or no damages. If, for example, a procedure was performed without the consent of the patient, no "harm" might have resulted; indeed the patient may be said to have benefitted. Nevertheless, an action lies in intentional tort for the patient having been deprived of his right to choose, and the absence of tangible damages is not fatal to the claim as would be the case in a negligence action.

Finally, an intentional act may subject the defendant to criminal as well as civil liability in some cases. The same case alleging lack of informed consent and thus civil assault and battery claims could also result in criminal charges of assault and battery, if appropriate. In other cases of intentional tort, a psychiatrist who breaches his duty of care to a patient by engaging in a sexual relationship with the patient exposes himself not only to an action for intentional tort, but in some jurisdictions, criminal liability. Because of the procedural and evidentiary consequences (positive and negative) of pleading a case in intentional tort, often malpractice plaintiffs will plead their cases in both negligence and intentional tort, or in the alternative. If both theories are presented, somewhat different facts may support each theory. If they are presented in the alternative (which is permitted by some, but not all, courts) the same facts can support both theories and the jury is left to sort out which, if any, causes of action have been proved on the basis of the evidence.

A. ASSAULT AND BATTERY

A battery occurs when an individual is subjected to non-consensual touching that is in some way harmful or offensive to him. An assault occurs when an individual is placed in a position where he is in reasonable fear of non-consensual touching which is harmful or offensive to him. If a person is hit over the head with a billy club, the assault is seeing the club directed at him and fearing that he will be hit, while the battery is actually being hit by the club. If the same person were hit over the head while sleeping, the claim of battery would still prevail, but the assault claim would lack the critical element of fear or apprehension.

Most cases of assault and battery in the medical malpractice context occur because a practitioner undertakes to perform a procedure without securing the necessary informed consent. See chapter 4. A medical procedure performed most skillfully will still amount to a battery if the patient did not agree to it or would not have agreed had he been adequately informed about it. Alternatively, in some cases battery is alleged because although the patient consented to treatment, the treatment went beyond the scope of the consent. In *Schloendorff v. Society of New York Hospital* (N.Y.1914), a patient who allegedly consented to examination under ether brought an action in intentional tort against the physician because the physician performed a subsequent operation for which there had been no prior agreement. More recently, in *Perna v. Pirozzi* (N.J. 1983), a patient brought suit in intentional tort because she had consented to an operation to be performed by one surgeon and it was thereafter performed by another physician. The vast majority of assault and battery cases that are brought against medical practitioners occur in the context of inadequate consent.

Occasionally cases are brought in intentional tort against medical personnel who employ measures intended to restrain patients for medical treatment. Occasionally psychiatric personnel, for example, will need to use physical force to restrain a patient, and thereafter may be sued for undue force. These cases are generally decided upon the facts of the individual case as to whether the nature of the force was reasonable and warranted under the circumstances. A variation on that theme occurred in *Mattocks v. Bell* (D.C.App.1963). In this case, a two year old child was being treated by a medical student for a lacerated tongue. During the procedure the child bit down on the student's finger and would not release it. After several unsuccessful efforts to free his finger, the student struck the child on the cheek. In a subsequent action for intentional tort, the court held that the amount of force was proper under the circumstances, therefore negating any liability.

An increasingly large number of plaintiffs have brought malpractice actions against practitioners, notably mental health professionals, for battery as a consequence of engaging the plaintiffs in sexual activity during, after, or as a part of, treatment. It is consistently held, particularly in the context of mental health treatment, that it is completely improper and unethical for a practitioner to suggest, agree or in any other way participate in a sexual relationship with a current patient. Often, it is considered improper to engage in sexual relations with former patients as well. Eleven states impose criminal penalties for such conduct and virtually all states recognize it to be the basis for a civil action. See West's Fla. Stat. Ann. § 491.0112 (1991). A growing number of states have specific statutes that give rise to the civil action. See Ill. Ann. Stat. ch. 740, ¶ 14 (Smith–Hurd 1993) (P.A. 85–1254 § 1, eff. Jan. 1, 1989). The more difficult question is whether such actions should be pled in negligence or intentional tort.

In *Simmons v. United States* (9th Cir.1986), the court explained the theory under which cases of sexual exploitation are deemed to constitute negligence. In short, psychiatric patients often develop an attachment to, and a dependence upon, the doctor as an intended consequence of the treatment. Known as transference reactions, therapy patients routinely develop strong feelings toward the therapist that make them vulnerable to abuse by an unethical therapist who exploits the power and position that arises by virtue of the transference process. Thus in *Simmons,* the court held that the therapist's sexual abuse of the patient constituted a mishandling of the transference reaction and, therefore, professional negligence. Even though the standard defense to exploitation is consent of the patient (which may, in fact, have been the case), the literature and the cases clearly indicate that the consent of such a patient is invalid because of the involuntary transference reaction and the coercive nature of the relationship.

In earlier cases alleging sexual exploitation, plaintiffs were faced with the dilemma of whether to plead their case in intentional tort (assault and battery, criminal conversation, alienation of affections) which seemed to best define the wrong and did not require the court to understand and willingly apply the transference principles to establish negligence. The problem with pleading in intentional tort was that professional liability carriers would generally disclaim coverage for those acts which did not seemingly arise out of the professional treatment. The alternative, of course, was to allege that the sexual activity did arise out of treatment, and to attempt to prove that it resulted from the malpractice of the practitioner.

Much of the dilemma has been eliminated by two recent changes. First, today a growing number of courts now recognize the true nature of the exploitation claim, and this eliminates the barriers for plaintiffs to establish that they were wrongfully treated. In fact, the existence of civil and criminal penalties in some states demonstrates that exploitation is certainly not a consensual undertaking. Secondly, today, professional liability carriers routinely disclaim insurance coverage for sexual exploitation, regardless of how the matter is pleaded, so that the dilemma of how to present the case is no longer significant.

B. DEFAMATION

Defamation refers to the wrongful injury to reputation that is caused by communicating a false statement either orally (as in slander) or in writing (as in libel). In the context of medical practitioners, defamation can occur when a patient is wrongfully accused of having a certain disease (e.g., Acquired Immune Deficiency Syndrome (AIDS)), carrying a contagious condition (e.g., tuberculosis) or displaying a certain psychological or character flaw (e.g., paranoia). It is critical in proving a case of defamation that the communication be "published" (i.e., communicated to a third party) by the defendant alleged to have caused the defamation.

A medical practitioner alleged to have defamed another is not without defense. The most clear-cut defense is that the statement, although it may have caused injury, was nevertheless true. Thus truth is an absolute defense to defamation, although another tort such as invasion of privacy may occur if the information was privileged. Other defenses include privilege to communicate, such as when ordered to do so in the context of a judicial proceeding, even if the communication turns out to be false. Statements about patients made to other physicians for the purpose of discussing treatment (formally or informally) are also privileged, and a false statement about a patient in such a context does not amount to defamation.

Courts differ on the question of whether the defendant has to be negligent (or more, such as reckless) in communicating information which turns out to be false or whether an honest mistake in the knowledge about the truth of the matter will still support a claim of defamation. What is clear is that in the context of public figures or public officials, the defendant must either have actual knowledge or reckless disregard for the truth or falsity of the statement in order to be held accountable for defamation.

Sometimes statements are made that would otherwise be defamatory but are protected by a privilege or a qualified privilege in order to protect an important medical interest. For example, in *Simonsen v. Swenson* (Neb.1920), a physician received the results of a preliminary test which indicated that his patient had syphilis. Fearing that he might be contagious, the physician communicated the information to certain persons. It was eventually determined that the patient did not, in fact, have the disease, and that the physician's communication caused him harm. In the subsequent suit for defamation, however, the court declined to impose liability on the physician, holding that he had a duty to disclose the preliminary information and thus was protected in doing so.

C. FALSE IMPRISONMENT

False imprisonment is a tort which results when a person is intentionally detained in an unlawful manner or otherwise restricted in movement without privilege or consent of the individual. Among

the more common examples in the medical context
are patients who are not released from the hospital
because of failure to pay a bill or failure to sign
various forms for billing of third party payors. Another common example is the psychiatric patient or
non-psychiatric patient who demonstrates emotional problems and is wrongfully confined without
justifiable cause. A patient who has not been lawfully committed to an appropriate facility has no
obligation to stay, and physical or coercive efforts to
restrict movement may constitute false imprisonment. In *Marcus v. Liebman* (Ill.App.1978), a patient who voluntarily admitted herself to a general
hospital eventually wanted to leave. The physician,
who believed that she should stay, coerced her into
not leaving by threatening that if she did, he would
cause her to be committed to a state institution.
Upon those facts, the court determined that a jury
was entitled to decide whether the patient had
suffered false imprisonment.

A closely related cause of action that sometimes
occurs in the context of involuntary commitment is
abuse of process. This occurs when a physician,
without justifiable cause, participates in a judicial
proceeding to involuntarily commit or continue the
commitment of an individual in a psychiatric facility. In *Maniaci v. Marquette University* (Wis.1971),
a college freshman found to be leaving campus was
stopped from leaving by university officials by
means of initiating her commitment to a hospital.
In her subsequent lawsuit, the Wisconsin Supreme
Court ultimately found that while an action for

false imprisonment would not lie because the university had complied with legal procedures for involuntarily committing the student, there may have been a viable claim for abuse of process.

D. INVASION OF PRIVACY

Invasion of privacy occurs in the medical context when the legitimate privacy interests of patients are publicized to another person, whether or not the publicity casts the patient in some sort of derogatory light. Sometimes privacy interests are invaded by wrongful disclosure of confidential information, which will be discussed in the next section. Pure privacy claims, however, might be triggered by using, without permission, pictures that are taken of a patient during medical treatment or to demonstrate a particular result. In *Vassiliades v. Garfinckel's, Brooks Bros.* (D.C.App.1985), the defendant allegedly used "before" and "after" photographs of a patient's cosmetic surgery without obtaining her consent for their use. The plaintiff prevailed on theories of both invasion of privacy and breach of fiduciary obligation on the basis that she had suffered unwanted publicity in connection with the photographs.

The fact that the information revealed is truthful is not a defense to an invasion of privacy claim as it is to defamation claim. Nor is privilege generally successful in defending a claim. If, for example, a patient's case history is used for textbook or instructional purposes (rather than informal consultation) the patient is entitled to confidentiality. The name should not be revealed, nor should any readily identifying information that would cause the patient's identity to be known.

Physicians have sometimes been held liable for revealing private information about patients that is not necessarily expressly privileged nor disclosed as a consequence of the physician-patient relationship. For example, if a patient, while hospitalized, reveals to a physician a story about something that happened to her which is not pertinent to her treatment, but merely a personal tale, a theory of liability might be fashioned against the physician for invasion of privacy, even if the communication was not privileged.

E.   MISREPRESENTATION

A physician who negligently or intentionally misstates or conceals an important fact concerning a patient for the purpose of influencing treatment decisions or concealing treatment results may be liable for misrepresentation. Misrepresentation is closely related to another intentional tort, fraud, which may occur when a physician intentionally conceals an important fact concerning treatment that might affect the outcome, or the actions of the patient following treatment. If, for example, a physician performs a procedure negligently and then conceals his negligence by misrepresenting the error to the patient, this may constitute both fraud and misrepresentation, and a subsequent action may lie for both claims. Misrepresentation may also occur if a patient falsely represents to an insurance carrier or third-party payor that a particular procedure has either been done or needs to be done.

In order to recover for the tort of misrepresentation, it is necessary to establish that the person to whom the misrepresentation was made relied upon it. In *Simcuski v. Saeli* (N.Y.1978), the plaintiff claimed misrepresentation upon evidence that the defendant physician, knowing that the patient suffered post-operative problems as a result of the negligent manner that he performed surgery, nevertheless allowed her to think that the difficulties were transient and concealed the fact that there was treatment for the problems she suffered.

F. DISCLOSURE OF CONFIDENTIAL INFORMATION

A physician who, without consent or other cause, discloses to another confidential information about a patient which was learned within the physician-patient relationship, may be liable for breach of confidentiality. See *Horne v. Patton* (Ala.1973); *MacDonald v. Clinger* (N.Y.A.D.1982). In addition, several state and federal statutes, including licensing statutes, protect the confidentiality of medical information. See, e.g., Drug Abuse and Treatment Acts and Alcohol Prevention, Treatment and Rehabilitation Act, 42 U.S.C.A. §§ 290dd–3, 390ee–3 (West 1982 & Supp. 1986).

The reasons for confidentiality in the physician-patient relationship are straightforward. Medical treatment is often a private matter, during which patients discuss private and confidential issues with their physicians. In order to obtain the best possible care, patients need to be free to openly discuss all matters that relate to their care and treatment. Some issues may be highly sensitive or even embarrassing, while others may harm the patient if revealed. The ability of the patient to speak candidly requires that confidentiality be maintained. Statutes regulating licensing and testimonial privileges have sometimes been cited for the proposition that a cause of action exists for breach of confidentiality. Statutes concerning testimonial privileges generally hold that disclosure of confidential information is prohibited, even in the context of a judicial proceeding, unless the court first determines in the interest of justice that the privilege is waived.

In those cases in which a patient seeks the services of a physician for reasons other than medical treatment, the confidentiality of the relationship is qualified. Thus if a patient who claims workers' compensation is sent to the adverse party's physician to determine if the claim is warranted, the result of the examination is probably not privileged, at least as to the party seeking the examination. Similarly, if an employer or a life insurance company sends a candidate for a medical examination, the results of the examination will not be privileged as against the party requiring the patient to undergo the exam. See *Millsaps v. Bankers Life Co.* (Ill. App.1976).

By the same token, a plaintiff who places her medical condition into issue by virtue of filing a lawsuit and claiming damages impliedly waives the testimonial privilege that would prevent a physician from testifying. See *Bond v. District Court* (Colo. 1984) (seeking reversal of a discovery order pertaining to the treatment notes of a therapist where patient had put her mental pain and suffering into issue). Furthermore, as indicated earlier, physicians routinely consult one another informally to discuss patient care, exchanging information and discussing treatment plans. Generally no liability arises even though the identity of the patient may be disclosed.

In some cases, a patient's spouse is entitled (by statute or case law) to certain information about a patient, particularly under circumstances that it is necessary to protect the spouse. Similarly, sometimes parents or other family members are entitled to access certain information. By the same token, if a patient presents a danger of imminent threat to a third person, a physician may have an obligation to protect the third person, either by confining the dangerous person or warning the target of his aggressions. See *Tarasoff v. Regents of the University of California* (Cal.1976) and its progeny, supra at Chapter 2.

Under some circumstances, a physician is required to disclose otherwise confidential information by virtue of statutory mandatory reporting requirements. In cases of child abuse, gunshot wounds, contagious diseases and certain other matters, physicians are both obligated to report such findings and immunized from liability for disclosure of related confidential information. Nevertheless, the disclosure is limited to the information required to carry out the intent of the reporting requirements, and should not be abused to the extent that there is disclosure of peripheral information. Some courts have held that because the privilege of disclosure is conditional, it is abused if the information is either intentionally false or communicated with reckless disregard for its truth. The privilege is not lost if the disclosure is made in good faith, even though the information turns out to be false. Most courts will also maintain the privilege for mere negligence in disclosure.

II. EMOTIONAL DISTRESS AND OUTRAGE

When a medical practitioner acts in such a manner that is extreme and outrageous, and in so doing causes emotional distress, an independent tort may be alleged. Infliction of emotional distress can be alleged to be either negligent or intentional. It is not always easy in any particular case to determine how and when a jury will conclude that the infliction of emotional distress was negligent or intentional. In general, conduct that is extreme and outrageous or reckless is intentional while less cul-

pable conduct that also causes emotional distress
may be negligent.

Often the characterization as "negligent" or "intentional" is critical because of statutory or procedural implications. As previously mentioned, often
liability coverage is jeopardized in cases of intentional wrongdoing. If so, the characterization may
affect the availability of coverage. Furthermore,
many courts hold that if the conduct was negligent,
it must have produced some sort of physical manifestation (post-traumatic stress disorder, cardiac
arrest, etc.); if, however, the conduct was extreme
and outrageous, the requirement of physical manifestation is eliminated.

In those cases in which the person claiming emotional distress is not the patient but instead a
"bystander" who witnesses the injury of another,
courts typically hold that the "test" of recovery for
emotional distress is whether the distress to the
bystander was "foreseeable" as a consequence of
the alleged conduct. In *Thing v. La Chusa* (Cal.
1989), the court held that "foreseeability" was a
function of whether the plaintiff (1) was closely
related to the injury victim; (2) was present at the
scene of the injury and aware of the harm; and (3)
as a result suffered the type of severe emotional
harm that would be normally anticipated as a consequences of the circumstances.

The "foreseeability" approach was used in *Johnson v. Ruark Obstetrics and Gynecology Associates,
P.A.* (N.C.1990), where expectant parents of a still-

born fetus alleged that they observed the events that led to the death of their fetus. On a motion to dismiss, the court allowed the claim of negligent infliction of emotional distress to go forward on grounds of reasonable foreseeability. This approach is often used for claims of emotional distress by bystanders who witness injury to a loved one and would be expected to suffer harm as a result.

A number of courts have articulated the need for the bystander to be within a "zone of danger" in order to recover for emotional distress. In *Whethan v. Bismarck Hosp.* (N.D.1972), a mother who allegedly observed her newborn infant being dropped was considered to be within the zone of danger and thus able to fear that his safety was in jeopardy. Other courts, however, reject the zone of danger requirement, holding that recovery would be permitted if the bystander was present, observed the injury, was closely related to the patient and suffered emotional consequences as a result. On the other hand, in at least one case, a bystander was denied recovery because he was a "voluntary" witness to the occurrence. Thus in *Justus v. Atchison* (Cal.1977), a father who chose to be present in the delivery room was denied recovery as a bystander when complications arose that allegedly resulted in the death of his child. Having voluntarily undertaken to observe in the delivery room, he no longer qualified as a bystander who happened to witness an injury. The broad holding in *Justus* was qualified, however, in *Ochoa v. Superior Court* (Cal. 1985). The court determined that the voluntary or involuntary presence of the plaintiff should not be the decisive factor in determining whether the plaintiff may recover.

Furthermore, if there exists a contractual relationship between the parties and it becomes the basis for the claim of emotional distress, some courts have held that the bystander need not have necessarily observed the events. In *Newton v. Kaiser Hospital* (Cal.App.1986), the parents of a handicapped newborn alleged that the child was born partially handicapped because the physician failed to deliver the child by caesarean section. Neither parent actually observed the delivery as the mother was unconscious and the father was not present. The court held that the physician's contractual obligation to deliver a healthy baby established his duty, and foreseeability was unnecessary to bring a claim for emotional distress.

Yet another line of cases in which a contractual relationship forms the basis for a claim of emotional distress is exemplified by *Mazza v. Huffaker* (N.C.App.1983). In that case, a psychiatrist who treated a patient for four years thereafter developed an intimate (sexual) relationship with the patient's wife. The standard of care for psychiatrists at that time strictly forbid such a relationship on the basis of the harm that it would cause to the patient. The psychiatrist was found liable both in malpractice and infliction of emotional distress on the basis of the contractual duty owed to the patient. See also *Rowe v. Bennett* (Me.1986), for the same holding under a similar set of circumstances.

The more difficult cases allegedly causing emotional distress are those in which a practitioner's neglect or unprofessional conduct causes harm to the patient. In these cases the harm is generally not caused by medical practice or malpractice, and often the claim is defended on that basis. Usually courts will find a basis for allowing such claims, however, often labelling them torts of "outrage" or similar terms. For example, in *Johnson v. Woman's Hospital* (Tenn.App.1975), a woman who had lost a child during a premature birth sought information regarding the disposition of the child's body. After encountering much difficulty in ascertaining what had happened to the child's body, the mother was eventually directed to a hospital employee who presented to her a jar of formaldehyde containing the body of the infant. The court held that such action would clearly sustain the mother's claim of outrage.

In *Chew v. Paul D. Meyer, M.D., P.A.* (Md.App. 1987), the plaintiff presented to his physician an employment claim form to document his absence from work. He specifically told the physician that it had to be completed and returned to his employer promptly, or he could lose his job. Despite repeated inquiries, however, eighteen days elapsed before the form was returned, and the plaintiff lost his job as a result. The court allowed the plaintiff's action to go forward on the basis that the defendant had undertaken a contractual duty to the patient, and that his failure to perform resulted in damages to the plaintiff. Thus although the underlying claim was not one of medical negligence, the claim of mental distress was nevertheless supported.

There have been some cases in which the medical practitioner's unprofessional conduct served as the basis for the claim of emotional distress. In *Anderson v. Prease* (D.C.App.1982), the defendant was alleged to have screamed and cursed at the plaintiff, insisting that she leave his office. Finding that a viable claim existed, the court noted that the physician apparently knew that the plaintiff had a nervous condition that could make her particularly vulnerable to emotional distress as a consequence of those actions.

III. VIOLATION OF CIVIL RIGHTS

There have been numerous contexts in which medical malpractice plaintiffs have alleged that their civil rights have been violated. Both the federal Civil Rights Act and its state counterparts have been invoked to cover medical practices and physician's services. In some cases, plaintiffs have alleged discrimination in their access to services on the basis of race or national origin. In other cases, plaintiffs have cited specific statutory authority which has been developed to assist patients in exercising their civil rights. For example, in *Reid v. Indianapolis Osteopathic Medical Hosp., Inc.* (S.D.Ind.1989), the plaintiff brought an action under 42 U.S.C.A. § 1395dd, which is a federal statute designed to deter hospitals from "dumping" patients in need of medical care because of the patients' inability to pay. The statute seems to give such plaintiffs a private right of action and to recover damages in accordance with the malpractice laws of the state in which the hospital is located. See Chapter 8.

In *Leach v. Drummond Medical Group,* supra at chapter 1, patients who were part of a medical group were denied services because they filed a complaint with the medical licensing board against the group of physicians serving them. In their subsequent suit to compel the medical group to provide treatment, the court held that the plaintiffs had stated a cause of action under the state's Civil Rights Act, and that the physicians' refusal to treat the patients constituted arbitrary discrimination in violation of the statute. A complete analysis of the civil rights acts and related legislation and their applicability to potential claims of malpractice plaintiffs is beyond the scope of this book.

Yet another line of cases that have alleged "intentional" violation of civil rights are those involving the involuntary commitment of psychiatric patients, as well as the forcible administration of anti-psychotic medication in order to manage such patients once they are committed. Specific statutory guidelines exist for involuntary commitment, and failure to adhere to such guidelines has been held to infringe on the civil rights of those affected. Both federal and state civil rights acts have been invoked in order to enjoin the commitment and/or establish a private right of action for damages. See, e.g.,

Widgeon v. Eastern Shore Hospital Center (Md. 1984).

Finally, there is a growing number of cases brought primarily against mental health professionals who become sexually involved with their patients. A number of cases have been brought, typically under either a specific statute or under a malpractice theory. See *Simmons v. United States*, supra; *Mazza v. Huffaker*, supra. To the extent that a civil rights act is held to cover medical practices, a cause of action may also exist for sexual exploitation as a violation of civil rights.

CHAPTER FOUR

INFORMED DECISION MAKING

I. IN GENERAL: BATTERY
VS. NEGLIGENCE

The modern doctrine of informed consent is a logical outgrowth of the common law concept of battery, which is defined as an unlawful, non-consensual touching. Battery theory has been used in the health care law field to impose liability on a health care provider who performs a procedure without first obtaining the informed consent of his or her patient. Over time, negligence theory has replaced common law battery as the basis for litigation. Most of the modern cases involving informed consent address the question of whether or not the physician provided sufficient information to the patient; these cases focus on the quantity and quality of that information. It is unusual, but not impossible, for a case to arise today in which no consent at all was given. Procedures performed by physicians or other health care providers involve a touching of a patient's body. The law protects the right of a person not to be touched without consent and authorization. This concept is well rooted in common law as well as American constitutional law. The right of self-determination was articulated by Justice Cardozo in his opinion in the case of *Schloen-dorff v. Society of New York Hospital* (N.Y.1914):

> Every human being of adult years and sound mind has a right to determine what shall be done with his own body, and a surgeon who performs an operation without his patient's consent commits an assault for which he is liable in damages.

More recently, this concept was found to be an underpinning in the constitutional right to privacy. See *Griswold v. Connecticut* (S.Ct.1965); *Roe v. Wade* (S.Ct.1973), *Hondroulis v. Schumacher* (La. 1988).

There are two types of cases involving informed consent. The first type, and the one that is seen in most courts today, is the negligence case. In a negligence case, the question is whether the patient received enough information when consent was being sought and was obtained.

The second type of case, the assault and battery case, deals with whether or not consent was given at all.

The assault and battery cases may involve one or more of the following:

1. No consent at all was obtained;

2. A procedure completely or substantially different from the one authorized was performed;

3. The procedure exceeded the scope of the consent obtained.

Although the theories of battery and negligence may appear similar in many respects, there are differences which may have a dramatic effect on the pending action. One such difference is the statute of limitations. In some jurisdictions, the statute of limitations for battery cases is different from that for negligence cases. Other jurisdictions have enacted statutes applying to all actions against health care providers, in effect making the statute of limitations the same whether the action is filed under a battery or negligence theory. (See Massachusetts General Laws, Chapter 260, section 4.)

Another difference between the battery theory and the negligence theory relates to damages. In a negligence action, the successful plaintiff is entitled to recover compensatory damages resulting from the physician's failure to disclose certain risks which materialized. In a battery action, the successful plaintiff may recover for the unlawful touching, for all injuries resulting from the unlawful touching and, possibly, punitive damages.

II. PATIENT'S RIGHT TO INFORMATION

In order for a physician to lawfully perform a medical procedure on a patient, the patient must have in some manner consented to the treatment. The most common example of consent is when the patient is willing to undergo specific medical treatment and expresses this to the doctor. The requirement of consent may easily be fulfilled by such a willing and overt action by the patient. See Restatement (Second) of Torts § 892 and comment b.

A.   CONSENT: A BASIC REQUIREMENT

There are many ways in which the patient can express his consent to the treating physician, including written or oral manifestation by the patient. The limits of express consent and authorization by the patient are usually clear and easy to identify. A written consent form is an important tool and may even be required in some jurisdictions. See West's Fla. Stat. Ann. § 768.46 (1975); Ohio Rev. Code § 2317.54 (Baldwin 1977). A good consent form should include at least the following provisions;

1.   Patient's name.

2.   Date and time of consent.

3.   The patient's condition or problem, preferably in nontechnical language.

4.   Nature and purpose of the proposed procedure, preferably in non-technical language.

5.   Name of the physician who explained the proposed procedure and is obtaining consent.

6.   All material risks of the proposed procedure.

7.   Treatment alternatives, including non-treatment.

8.   Prognosis and risks of treatment alternatives, including non-treatment.

9.   Disclaimer of any warranty or guaranty of success.

10.   Identification of the physician who will perform the procedure, if different from the physician obtaining consent.

11.   The consent of the patient to the procedure.

12.   The consent of the patient to allow the physician to deviate or modify the procedure if unforeseen circumstances arise during the course of the procedure.

13.   An acknowledgment that the patient has been given the opportunity to ask questions and that any questions have been answered.

14.   Consent to disposal of removed organs and tissue.

15.   Signature of patient or legal guardian and a witness.

See *Hondroulis v. Schumacher* (La.1988). (Consent form tracking state statute established a rebuttable presumption of consent).

Unless the doctor and patient are in a jurisdiction where written consent is required, unwritten or oral consent may also be valid. This has its roots in an old Massachusetts case, *O'Brien v. Cunard S.S. Co.* (Mass.1891). The Supreme Judicial Court of Massachusetts held that the plaintiff consented to vaccination by standing in a line and holding out her arm to a doctor who was vaccinating passengers on a ship. The court stated that silence implies consent if the circumstances are such that a reasonable person would speak if the person had an objec-

tion.   Although oral consent may be upheld as
valid, in terms of clear proof, a writing is preferred.

There are other ways that the patient may consent without overtly manifesting her willingness to
the doctor.   The patient may actually be unwilling
to partake in the treatment, yet, the requirements
of proper informed consent may be fulfilled.   An
example of this is the principle of implied consent,
infra.

If a patient exhibits certain conduct that would
indicate that he or she is willing to undergo a
medical procedure, regardless of the patient's state
of mind or tacit unwillingness to undergo the treatment, the patient can be deemed to have consented
to the treatment.   Restatement (Second) of Torts
§ 892 and comment c.   This is only true if the
doctor reasonably understands that the patient's
conduct signifies consent.   The doctor also must act
in good faith in concluding that the patient's conduct accurately reflects a willingness by the patient
to undergo the medical treatment.

Traditionally, courts have deemed minors incompetent to give consent to medical treatment if they
are "unemancipated."   In such cases, consent of a
parent or guardian generally should be obtained
before procedures are performed on the minor.   See
Zoski v. Gaines (Mich.1935).   Of course, during an
emergency situation when the child's life is at
stake, or serious bodily harm may occur, the doctor
may perform a procedure on the patient without
consent.   Some jurisdictions have statutes which

grant immunity for physicians, dentists and hospitals which do not obtain the consent of a parent, legal guardian or other person having custody of a minor child when emergency treatment is necessary. See Mass. Gen. Laws Ch. 112, § 12F.

Maturity of the minor appears to have some effect on courts in some jurisdictions. That is, if a simple and beneficial procedure is to be performed and the child's parents cannot be reached, the doctor may proceed on the minor's consent, if the minor is deemed mature enough to make such a decision. See *Younts v. St. Francis Hosp. and School of Nursing, Inc.* (Kan.1970). In fact, one court has held that if the minor is a "mature minor" the minor's consent as well as the parents' consent is needed. See *Belcher v. Charleston Area Medical Ctr.* (W.Va. 1992).

"Emancipated" minors, or minors who have left their parents' control by marrying, entering military service or by other means, are, in some jurisdictions, given the right to give consent to medical or dental treatment without parental consent. See Mass. Gen. Laws Ch. 112, § 12F.

During the past twenty years or so, many courts, including the Supreme Court of the United States, have allowed minors faced with what traditionally have been termed "adult problems" to consent to treatment without parental consent. Examples of these situations include treatment of alcohol or drug addictions, treatment of sexually transmitted diseases, treatment following rape, prescription of birth control pills, and treatment concerning the minor's own child. *Cardwell v. Bechtol* (Tenn. 1987).

The right to an abortion including the rights of minors have been debated since the seminal case on abortion, *Roe v. Wade* (S.Ct.) was decided in 1973. The issue of parental consent to a minor child's having an abortion was raised three years later in the case of *Planned Parenthood of Central Mo. v. Danforth* (S.Ct.1976). In *Danforth*, the Supreme Court held unconstitutional the requirement that all minors obtain parental consent before having an abortion. The issue is still lingering, and other cases hold that parental consent may be required in certain cases, so long as there is a alternative procedure allowing the minor to seek authorization through the judicial process. See *Bellotti v. Baird* (S.Ct.1979) (requiring a judicial by-pass mechanism); *H.L. v. Matheson* (S.Ct.1981) (parental notice permitted under Utah law, but parents have no veto power.)

B. SCOPE OF CONSENT

Once the patient consents to the treatment, there is still a question as to the extent of the consent. Traditionally, physicians may not expand the scope of a patient's consent, as for example, in performing a related procedure. See *Mohr v. Williams* (Minn. 1905) and *Perry v. Hodgson* (Ga.1929). However, there are exceptions. When a physician, during the course of an operation, thinks that further action must be taken without delay in order to preserve the patient's life or save her from serious harm, then the scope may be expanded. See *Preston v. Hubbell* (Cal.App.1948).

Courts have also allowed a physician to use his or her reasonable judgment in expanding the scope of the operation. That is, if an unforeseen problem arises while the physician is performing a procedure which requires additional treatment, and a patient is unable to give consent, then the doctor may expand the scope of the original consent in order to deal with the problem. Again, some courts have held that doctors may only do this in emergency situations. See *Danielson v. Roche* (Cal.App.1952); *Rothe v. Hull* (Mo.1944). In *Mohr*, supra, that court held a doctor's decision to perform a procedure on the patient's left ear was actionable where the patient's consent was only for the right ear; even though the court found that the condition was serious, it was not an emergency. Contra, *Buzzell v. Libi* (N.D.1983).

In other jurisdictions, courts have held that, under the extension doctrine, a care-giver may expand the scope of the patient's consent in certain situations. It is based on the notion that "no reasonable person would object if in a position to make a decision." See W. Keeton. D. Dobbs, R. Keeton & D. Owen, Prosser & Keeton on the Law of Torts § 18: at 117–8 (5th ed. 1984).

The extension doctrine was applied in a 1956 North Carolina case to absolve from liability a physician who performed an additional procedure. *Kennedy v. Parrott* (N.C.1956). The physician, during the course of an appendectomy, discovered and punctured some ovarian cysts which he found, without gaining the patient's consent first. The Supreme Court of North Carolina held that the patient could not give consent, the condition could not have been diagnosed prior to treatment, there was no indication that the patient would not consent to the procedure, the extension was in the area of the original incision, and there was sound medical justification for extending the authorized surgery. Accordingly, the physician incurred no liability.

C. IMPLIED OR SUBSTITUTED CONSENT

If a person is brought into a hospital or doctor's office unconscious, with injuries that appear to be life-threatening, medical personnel may provide that person with treatment, even though that person is unable to consent. The concept that allows the provider to act without express consent is the legal fiction known as "implied consent." The theory behind implied consent is that it is in the public interest to have medical personnel provide care to dying patients or patients with life-threatening conditions without fear of legal action. See *Hernandez v. United States* (D.Kan.1979); *Jackovach v. Yocom* (Iowa 1931). Implied consent has been held to exist even in non-emergent situations. See *O'Brien v. Cunard S.S. Co., Ltd.* (Mass.1891). (Holding out one's arm, consent to vaccination).

When a person cannot, or is not competent to, give consent to medical treatment, the law generally allows for the patient's relatives or guardian to give consent for the patient. This theory is known as substituted consent. See *In re Estate of Longeway* (Ill.1989); and *In re Estate of Greenspan* (Ill.1990).

Much of the case law surrounding substituted consent arises out of the parent-and-child relationship. In many jurisdictions, minors are considered incapable to consent to treatment and the surrogate decision-maker will more often than not be a parent or guardian. Generally, it is appropriate for the parent to make a medical choice for a child who cannot; however, that parent also must possess the mental capacity to give consent or withhold consent to treatment.

Recently, courts have held that a parent could not force a child to go through a medical procedure that is not in the child's best interest and is against the wishes of the other parent. In the case of *Curran v. Bosze* (Ill.1990), the father of three and one-half year-old twins sought an order compelling the twins to submit to bone marrow harvesting so that they could donate bone marrow to their half brother who suffered from leukemia. This was against the wishes of the twins' mother. The court ruled in favor of the mother and held that (1) the doctrine of substituted consent did not apply and (2) the bone marrow harvesting was not in the best interests of the twins.

Substituted consent should be distinguished from the doctrine of substituted judgment which is used quite frequently with regard to patients who are comatose or otherwise unable to communicate. Substituted judgment authorizes a surrogate decision-maker to make treatment decisions on behalf of an individual who lacks capacity to do so. The surrogate must "establish, with as much accuracy as possible, what decision the patient would make if [the patient] were competent to do so." *Longeway*, supra.

The role of the surrogate decision-maker has changed in recent years with the passage of statutes allowing a "living will" or a "health care proxy." These statutes allow patients to document in advance their wishes in a living will or in a health care proxy. Patients can articulate through these documents when and if they would like to withhold or withdraw life-sustaining procedures, or to designate someone to make decisions for them. In the absence of one of these "advance directives", the surrogate decision-maker must "determine with as much accuracy as possible, the wants and needs of the person involved." See *Brophy v. New England Sinai Hospital* (Mass.1986).

Generally, if a situation is not life-threatening, a patient may refuse treatment if he or she is competent to do so. *Riggins v. Nevada* (S.Ct.1992). (It was error to order that a person charged with murder be administered antipsychotic drugs during his trial over his objection). But even when a patient is conscious and competent, some courts are reluctant to allow the patient to refuse "non-heroic" life-saving measures. See *Matter of Storar* (N.Y. 1981).

For incompetent patients sustained by artificial life support with virtually no chance of recovery, courts have held that the life support may be withdrawn at the request of the incompetent patient's guardians when there is sufficient evidence to establish that the patient, if competent, would have requested withdrawal. See *Matter of Quinlan* (N.J. 1976); *Brophy v. New England Sinai Hospital, Inc.* (Mass.1986) and *Cruzan v. Dir., Missouri Dept. of Health* (S.Ct.1990). (In *Cruzan*, the Supreme Court recognized the right of a person to refuse treatment, but held that a State may impose reasonable restrictions on that right, such as requiring the petitioners to establish the wishes of the now-incompetent patient by a higher standard of proof than a preponderance of the evidence.)

D. INFORMED CONSENT

Not only must consent be given by the patient to the caregiver, but such consent must be informed. That is to say, certain information about the medical procedure, its risks and benefits, its costs and side effects, must be made available to the patient before consent is given. Informed consent is designed to give the patient the information needed in order for him or her to make a decision that reflects the wishes of the patient. This provides the patient with autonomy and self-determination. Courts have recognized that informed consent involves more than simply obtaining the signature of a patient on a form. It is, in effect, a process, involving a dialogue between the health care provider and the patient. For example, in a discussion of the nature of informed consent, the Maryland court said in *Sard v. Hardy* (Md.1977):

> The doctrine of informed consent ... follows logically from the universally recognized rule that a physician, treating a mentally competent adult under non-emergency circumstances, cannot properly undertake to perform surgery or administer other therapy without the prior consent of his patient. In order for the patient's consent to be effective, it must have been an "informed consent," one that is given after the patient has received a fair and reasonable explanation of the contemplated treatment or procedure.

It follows that if the health care provider does not make the necessary disclosures and does not receive the patient's "informed consent," he or she is exposed to liability for malpractice.

III. INFORMED REFUSAL OF TREATMENT

A patient has the right to refuse, as well as consent, to treatment. The right to refuse treatment also has its roots in the right of self-determination and the right of privacy as interpreted through the first and fourteenth amendments to the Constitution.

Informed refusal of treatment requires that a physician communicate that information which a reasonable patient would require in order to make an "informed" judgment about whether to consent to treatment. Such information includes the risks and benefits of a proposed treatment, as well as the available alternatives. Furthermore, as part of the physician-patient relationship, the physician also incurs an obligation to disclose to the patient the consequences of failing to undergo a recommended medical procedure, and can be held liable in malpractice if he fails to do so.

In *Truman v. Thomas* (Cal.1980) a family practitioner recommended that a female patient of childbearing age undergo a routine pap smear, which tests for cervical cancer. Although he claims to have offered the procedure to his patient on several occasions, he never specifically advised her about the benefits of the procedure, and particularly the risks of failing to have the test. The patient refused the test, allegedly because of its cost, and later died of cervical cancer. The California Supreme Court held the physician liable on the basis that he failed to disclose a material risk of refusing the recommended procedure. In defining "material risk" the court identified that information "which the physician knows or should know would be regarded as significant by a reasonable person in the patient's position when deciding to accept or reject the recommended medical procedure."

Generally, when a medical condition is not life-threatening, a patient has a right to refuse treat-

ment, or choose a procedure other than that recommended, assuming the patient is competent to do
so.   There are exceptions to this rule, which are
beyond the scope of this discussion.   Generally, the
exceptions apply to the treatment of children whose
parent(s) or guardian refuse to consent to recommended procedures, and to competent adults whose
medical conditions pose a grave risk to life.   In the
latter, some courts have been willing to balance the
right of the patient to refuse treatment with the
right of a minor child, for example, whose well-
being would be significantly affected by the death of
a parent.   In *Norwood Hospital v. Munoz* (Mass.
1991) and *Public Health Trust of Dade County v.
Wons* (Fla.1989) competent adult patients, who
were Jehovah's Witnesses, refused life-saving blood
transfusions on the basis that receiving blood products was contrary to their religious beliefs.   The
courts held that the right of such adults to refuse
lifesaving treatment was not absolute, but would be
considered in light of other interests which the state
was obligated to promote.   Such interests included
the rights of their minor children to preserve a
parent's life, and in each case the patient's right to
refuse treatment *was* overridden.   Cases such as
Munoz and *Wons* are the exception, however, and
typically an informed patient may refuse treatment,
even when his or her condition is life-threatening.
In emergency situations and those in which the
competency of the patient is uncertain, physicians
may err on the side of providing treatment.

IV. THE DUTY OF DISCLOSURE

Although it is clear that the patient is entitled to obtain the information necessary to give an informed consent, the question sometimes arises as to who has the obligation to make the necessary disclosures. In particular, when more than one health care provider is involved, it is not always clear with whom the duty to disclose ultimately rests. In general, most courts will hold that the duty of disclosure remains with the physician who performs the medical procedure or provides the medical treatment, diagnostic tests or other medical care. See Rozovsky, Consent to Treatment: A Practical Guide, 2nd Ed. (Little, Brown & Co.1990); *Ritter v. Delaney* (Tex.App.1990). The health care facility is not generally responsible for obtaining informed consent unless it knew or had reason to know that the physician had not obtained the patient's consent. *Rozovsky* at 69. See also *Pauscher v. Iowa Methodist Med. Center* (Iowa 1987).

In cases where multiple physicians participate in the treatment of a patient, it is not always clear where the duty to obtained informed consent should lie. For example, if a physician requests a consultation and the consulting physician requires that certain tests be performed, generally it is only the consultant that is required to obtain consent. On the other hand, if a physician orders a procedure to be performed by another physician (such as a radiologist), it is possible that both physicians may incur the duty to obtain consent. See *Halley v.*

Birbiglia (Mass.1983).   The question of whether both physicians are responsible depends largely upon whether the second physician acted in the capacity of an assistant, or whether he was responsible for a discrete aspect of the treatment.   Cf. *Cornfeldt v. Tongen* (Minn.1977) (anesthesiologist and general surgeon both responsible for disclosure to the patient) with *Bell v. Umstattd* (Tex.App. 1966) (anesthesiologist not responsible for disclosure to the patient unless the patient makes specific inquiry of him).   Still other courts defer to the applicable standards of the profession to determine who has an obligation of disclosure.

A.   STANDARDS FOR DISCLOSURE

The law of informed consent must necessarily apply a standard to determine whether or not a physician provided the patient with enough information when the patient's consent was sought and obtained.   Historically, the test was the "professional standard" as articulated in the leading case of *Natanson v. Kline* (Kan.1960).   In *Nathanson*, the court stated that the duty to disclose was "limited to those disclosures which a reasonable medical practitioner would make under the same or similar circumstances."   In applying this standard, the plaintiff must present expert testimony from other physicians to show that the defendant did not provide as much information as a reasonable physician would have provided in the same situation.   See *Culbertson v. Mernitz* (Ind.1992).   The "same situation" requirement has been interpreted with some specificity. For example, some jurisdictions hold that if a doctor is practicing in a small town, he or she should only be held to the standard of doctors practicing in small towns, not large cities. See *Smith v. Weaver* (Neb.1987) and Neb.Rev.St. §§ 44–2801 et seq., 44–2816. With the advent of a more universal quality of health care, regardless of location, this specificity requirement may be diminishing.

Although the professional standard is still the standard in the majority of jurisdictions, there is a trend in this country toward what is known as the "material risk" standard or "reasonable patient" standard. This standard was adopted in such cases as *Canterbury v. Spence* (D.C.Cir.1972) and *Cobbs v. Grant* (Cal.1972). See also *Largey v. Rothman* (N.J.1988) and *Hondroulis v. Schumacher* (La. 1988). In both *Canterbury* and *Cobbs*, the courts found that the professional standard violated the patient's right of self-determination. The patient owns the right to determine what is to be done with his or her body. Thus, the focus should be on what information the patient requires to make a decision, rather than on what a reasonable physician would do under the circumstances. *Canterbury* held that in order for a patient to give informed consent, he or she must have all the "material" information regarding "the inherent and potential hazards of the proposed treatment, the alternatives to that treatment, if any, and the results likely if the patient remains untreated."

The *Canterbury* court defined materiality as follows:

A risk is thus material when a reasonable person, in what the physician knows or should know to be the patient's position, would be likely to attach significance to the risk or cluster of risks in deciding whether or not to forego the proposed therapy.

The test these courts applied is an objective test. In order for the plaintiff to prevail, she must establish that she would not have consented to the procedure had she been given sufficient information and that a reasonable person would likewise have refused.

Since the adoption of the material risk standard, the courts have struggled with the application of materiality test to fact patterns being litigated. Two factors the courts have weighed are the severity of the undisclosed risk and the incidence of harm. A consensus appears to be developing that the greater the severity, the more likely that the risk should be disclosed, even though the incidence of the materialized risk is quite small.

B. EXCEPTIONS TO THE DUTY TO DISCLOSE

In certain situations physicians have a right to proceed with treatment in the absence of the informed consent of the patient. The three major exceptions occur concern *(1) emergency, (2) waiver and (3) therapeutic privilege.*

In the event of a medical emergency, a physician is expected to render life-saving care to a patient whether or not the patient or a close relative is present to consent to treatment. A medical emergency is present when the life of the patient is threatened or when the failure to perform a certain procedure will reasonably result in a serious or permanent impairment or disfigurement to the patient. The patient is said to impliedly consent to treatment until such time as his or her condition is stabilized. See implied consent, supra at pp. 95–98 and the Good Samaritan statutes at pp. 146–149.

The patient's right to informed consent might also be waived under certain limited circumstances. When a patient determines that he knows or understands so little about the medical procedure in question and is in no position to make an informed judgment, or is under such stress that he is unable to make an informed judgment, or a language barrier exists that cannot be overcome by translation, some courts may consider that the patient has waived his right of informed consent. It is generally not acceptable, however, for a patient to blindly assert that he will not or cannot participate in the decision about whether to accept treatment, leaving the physician to act on his own. Furthermore, "[t]o waive the right of informed consent the patient must know he has the right. The patient needs to be aware of the doctor's duty to disclose, the patient's own right to make a decision either consenting or refusing, and that the doctor cannot do anything without his consent." Burwell, Informed Consent, 34 Med. Tr. Tech. Q. 439 (1988).

Under certain limited circumstances a physician may also have the right to withhold information that is pertinent to informed decision-making because the physician believes that disclosure would be harmful to the patient. This is therapeutic privilege. Thus if it reasonably appears that the required disclosure might so upset the patient that it would threaten his or her health or well-being, the physician may have the right to withhold such information or limit the scope of such information.

The standard for invoking the therapeutic privilege is a "reasonable practitioner" standard. See *Nishi v. Hartwell* (Haw.1970). Therapeutic privilege was also asserted in *Canterbury* where it was said to only be appropriate in such cases where it appears that risk disclosure poses such a threat of detriment to the patient as to become infeasible or contraindicated from a medical point of view. *Canterbury v. Spence* (D.C.Cir.1972). *Canterbury* also noted that even when the privilege is invoked, the physician must still provide the patient with information that is relevant and not harmful to the patient. Thus it is not a blanket privilege. See also *Salgo v. Leland Stanford Jr. University Board of Trustees* (Cal.App.1957).

Finally, a recent federal court held that under a particular circumstance where obtaining informed consent was "not feasible", the requirement would not be imposed. In *Doe v. Sullivan* (D.C.Cir.1991) the plaintiff alleged that the government, without informed consent, used unapproved investigational drugs on military personnel stationed in Saudi Arabia during the Gulf War. The court held that it would be impractical to obtain consent from all combat-ready personnel, and thus the informed consent requirement was not enforceable. This exception to the rule would likely not extend to situations not involving military readiness.

C. DUTY TO DISCLOSE ECONOMIC INTERESTS

Aside from the standard medical information that a doctor has a duty to disclose to the patient, other types of information also may have to be disclosed. Recently, courts have held that physicians have a duty to disclose any economic interest that a physician might have in a patient's tissue. This matter was discussed in the landmark case of *Moore v. Regents of The University of California* (Cal.1990). The plaintiff in this case had a rare form of cancer known as hair-cell leukemia. Because this disease was so rare, the plaintiff's cells and blood product was of great commercial value. During the ongoing doctor/patient relationship, the doctors were profiting financially by the use of the plaintiff's cells without ever revealing this to the plaintiff. Informed consent was neither sought nor given. The plaintiff sued on the theory of conversion, breach of fiduciary duty and lack of informed consent. The court held that the doctor had a fiduciary duty to his patient and that informed consent should have been sought by the doctors before entering into any activities in which they would profit from plaintiff's cells.   But it also ruled that there was no cause of action for conversion, saying that patients do not own the tissue removed from their bodies and have no right to share in the profits from the commercialization of such tissue.

D.   EXPERIMENTAL PROCEDURES

Courts have held that when a health care provider offers and experimental procedure to the patient, the provider has a duty to inform the patient of the experimental nature of the proposed procedure. See *Estrada v. Jaques* (N.C.App.1984) (steel coil embolization).

E.   HIV STATUS OF THE PHYSICIAN

With the advent of the AIDS epidemic, doctors are forced to consider a new aspect of informed consent and the duty to disclose.   They are faced with revealing to their patients that they, themselves, are infected with the virus.   In the case of *The Estate of William Behringer v. Medical Center at Princeton* (N.J.Super.1991), the court held that as a component of informed consent, the patient has a right to be told that his doctor is sero-positive for HIV (human immunodeficiency virus) before the doctor performs invasive procedures that might put the patient at risk.   The *Behringer* court reasoned that disclosure of the doctor's HIV status must be made whenever there is a material risk that a doctor may transmit the virus to his patient and that surgical or other invasive procedures pose such a risk.

Related to the topic of the HIV virus, a court has held that a physician had no duty to disclose to a patient the risk of contracting the HIV virus from a blood transfusion prior to 1985, because such a risk was not apparent prior to that date. The court said also that the physician had no duty to inform the patient of the possibility of providing for an autologous transfusion or self-donation. See *Doe v. Johnston* (Iowa 1991).

F.   AFTER–DISCOVERED DANGERS

Doctors may also have a duty to disclose after discovered dangers. That is, if a doctor discovers after a procedure that a patient might be at risk, the doctor has a duty to disclose such information. See *Tresemer v. Barke* (Cal.App.1978) (gynecologist owed a duty to warn patient of dangers of intrauterine device, when doctor obtained new knowledge of its dangers).

V.   THE REQUIREMENT OF CAUSATION

Once a plaintiff is able to establish that a physician acted, or failed to act, without the requisite consent, the plaintiff must still prove that the ab-

sence of informed consent is causally related to an
identifiable harm.   Like all negligence actions,
those premised upon failure of informed consent
also require proof of causation.   In general, the
plaintiff must establish that had the necessary information been provided, he or she would have
acted differently or expected a different outcome.

In determining whether a different outcome
would have occurred had the required information
been disclosed, a number of different "tests" or
"standards" have been used.   A majority of jurisdictions use an objective or "reasonable person"
standard in which the plaintiff must establish that
the reasonable person, having be given the necessary information, would have refused (or accepted)
the proposed treatment.   See Rozovsky, Consent to
Treatment: A Practical Guide, 2nd Ed. (Little,
Brown & Co.1990) at 79.   See also *Pardy v. United
States* (7th Cir.1986).

An alternative to the objective test is the "subjective" or "actual patient" test.   Those jurisdictions
which apply this standard would allow a particular
plaintiff to establish that although the reasonable
person might not have acted differently had the
necessary information been disclosed, he or she
would have on the basis of some individual character or personality trait or experience.   See *Arena v.
Gingrich* (Or.1988).   The standard of proof can
vary, but proof of a subjective reason for believing
that one would act contrary to that of the reasonable person might require clear and convincing evidence.

Yet another alternative is for the court to require that both the objective and subjective standards be satisfied. This might minimize the likelihood that a patient, observing through hindsight, would opt for a different result. See *Harnish v. Children's Hospital* (Mass.1982). If both standards are required, a physician can avoid liability if the plaintiff cannot show that even if the reasonable person would have acted in particular way, he or she would also have so acted. The outcome-determinative element of causation, particularly when observed on an objective basis, makes it difficult to establish that the absence of informed consent "caused" the patient's injury.

Many courts require a further element of causation when a patient alleges that a risk of a certain treatment was not adequately disclosed, and that had disclosure been made, the procedure would have been refused. They require that the risk complained of actually materialize. See *Canterbury v. Spence* (D.C.Cir.1972). In *Canterbury*, the physician allegedly failed to disclose that paralysis was a risk of a laminectomy procedure, and that failure to disclose that risk violated the physician's duty of care. Furthermore, had such a risk been disclosed, the patient alleged that he would have refused the procedure. After the procedure, the plaintiff was paralyzed, and the physician was held liable.

Finally, courts generally require that any injury that results after nondisclosure of a material risk be proximately caused by the medical treatment or procedure. Thus if paralysis is a material risk of a laminectomy procedure, and paralysis results, it must still be proved that it was the laminectomy that caused the paralysis.

VI. FRAUDULENT MISREPRESENTATION AND CONCEALMENT

Informed consent can be voided by fraudulent misrepresentation and concealment or non-disclosure of information by the doctor. An action for intentional misrepresentation may be maintained if (1) a false statement of material fact is made; (2) the misrepresentation is made by a party who knows or believes the statement is false; (3) the party intends to induce another to act; (4) action by the other is made in reliance on the statement's truth; and (5) injury to the patient results from said reliance. *Smith v. Kurtzman* (Ill.App.1988). The requirements for a successful action based on misrepresentation are substantially the same as for ordinary negligence cases except that in the former, the act is done intentionally. See *Bloskas v. Murray* (Colo.1982).

In another case, the court held that a professional football player had been the victim of misrepresentation. The player suffered a knee injury while in college and re-injured the knee during his professional career. The team doctor failed to reveal to him that he had a degenerative and irreversible knee injury and that continued professional play would only worsen the condition. *Krueger v. San*

Francisco Forty–Niners (Cal.App.1987). See also Restatement (Second) of Torts §§ 310–311, 525, 550, 552.

CHAPTER FIVE

CAUSATION AND DAMAGES

I. IN GENERAL: ESTABLISHING CAUSATION

A cause of action for negligence requires four elements: a duty based upon a standard of care; breach of that duty; causation; and damages. See Chapter 2. On the other hand, it is often said that a practitioner is negligent when he fails to adhere to the requisite standard of care. The distinction is that in order to maintain an actionable claim, the negligent act must also be causally related to an identifiable harm. The element of causation along with the existence of damages transforms substandard practice into an actionable claim.

The fact that there must be a causal connection between the substandard level of care and the harm that results is undisputed. The absence of such a connection will be fatal to a claim of malpractice. Thus in *Alfonso v. Lund* (10th Cir.1986) in which the plaintiff claimed that his two fingers which had been accidentally severed could have been reimplanted, the court held that the plaintiff must demonstrate the defendant's actions proximately caused the disability and disfigurement that he alleges: "The burden of proving with reasonable certainty the causal connection between the treatment complained of and the plaintiff's loss or injury rests on the plaintiff, and a judgment in a malpractice action based upon conjecture, surmise or speculation cannot be sustained...." See also *Paige v. Manuzak* (Md.App.1984) in which the court refused to hold a hospital liable for negligently administering penicillin post-operatively to an allergic patient because there was no proof that subsequent complications were proximately caused by the negligent use of the drug.

It is often said that there are two types of causation: cause-in-fact and proximate cause. If injury to the plaintiff would not have occurred "but for" the defendant's wrongful act, or if injury to the plaintiff was a foreseeable result of the defendant's act, it is said that the acts of the defendant were the cause-in-fact of the plaintiff's injury. Proximate cause, on the other hand, refers to whether, considering all other relevant factors, the act(s) of the defendant were the legal cause of the plaintiff's injury. For example, the defendant's act(s) may have been one factor but not necessarily the only factor. Proximate cause in that instance may depend upon whether the act(s) of the defendant were a significant factor in bringing about the plaintiff's injury. Alternatively, the acts of one person might set into motion certain events, but another's act might constitute a superseding cause which results in the plaintiff's injury. Thus the cause-in-fact is an important determination, but ultimately it is the proximate cause that determines the liability of the defendant.

Negligent acts and omissions are often said to be the cause of injury if they satisfy the "but for" test. Thus if it can be said that but for the acts of the defendant, the plaintiff would not have sustained his injury, it would be said that the defendant's actions were a cause of injury. On the other hand, the fact that the actions were a cause of injury might not result in his liability unless it is established that they were a substantial cause of injury. The recent New Hampshire case of *Peterson v. Gray* (N.H.1993) highlights the difficulty in using proximate cause as a determining factor for establishing liability. In that case a plaintiff with a preexisting condition engaged the defendant to perform hand surgery, but did not achieve a successful result. The court observed that ". . . if the jury determined that the plaintiff's [pre-existing condition] was 'a proximate cause' of [her result], then the defendant's actions could not possibly have been 'the proximate cause.'"

A. SUBSTANTIAL FACTOR

In *Mitchell v. Gonzales* (Cal.1991) the California Supreme Court rejected jury instructions on proximate cause on the basis that they were unduly confusing to the jury. Instead, it relied on whether the conduct of the defendant was a "contributing factor" of the plaintiff's injury. This goes beyond the "substantial factor" principles, but indicates that causation is not necessarily an all-or-nothing matter. The trier of fact must then determine to what extent the act contributed to the plaintiff's injury in deciding whether the defendant should be held liable.

B. SUPERSEDING CAUSE

In some cases the harm to a patient may have multiple causes, at least as determined by the "but for" test. For example, in *Siggers v. Barlow* (6th Cir.1990) an emergency room physician negligently diagnosed the plaintiff, failing to identify a fracture that required surgery. When the x-ray films were read by an attending physician, the fracture was identified and reported to a subsequent emergency room physician whose duty was to communicate the new diagnosis to the patient. The patient was never notified and suffered irreparable injury as a result. The court noted that under Kentucky law the question of whether the "superseding cause" constituted a legal cause was one for the court (as opposed to the jury) to determine. A superseding cause is defined as "an act of a third person or other force which by its intervention prevents the actor from being liable for harm to another which his antecedent negligence is a substantial factor in bringing about." Restatement (Second) of Torts § 440. The court concluded that the failure of a third person to prevent the harm caused by another person's negligence is not a superseding cause.

C. JOINT AND SEVERAL LIABILITY

Sometimes an injury is caused by the negligent acts of two or more persons who act in concert, resulting in the plaintiff's injury. If it appears that they acted together (rather than separately) and in so doing caused a single injury, they are usually considered to be "joint tortfeasors." The determination about whether to assess liability jointly is a decision for the trial court, and is likely to depend upon such factors as whether each defendant had a similar duty, whether the same facts and evidence will be used in the cases against each of them, and whether the injury to the plaintiff can be separated into aspects caused by each tortfeasor. See, e.g. *Riff v. Morgan Pharmacy* (Pa.Super.1986).

In the medical content, the alternative to practitioners acting together to cause injury to the plaintiff is the possibility that they act successively. In that case the subsequent practitioner might have either mitigated the damage of the first or corrected the problem before it affected the patient. For example, one physician might be negligent in his initial diagnosis or treatment of a problem, and a subsequent practitioner fails to identify and correct it, perhaps resulting in an exacerbation of the original symptoms. Who is liable, and for what?

The first practitioner who was negligent in diagnosing and treating the problem is potentially liable not only for all foreseeable consequences as a result of his own negligence, but also for the foreseeable consequences of the negligence of the subsequent practitioner. See 1 D. Louisell and H. Williams, Medical Malpractice 16.06 (1986). When there are successive acts of negligence by two or more tortfeasors, they are generally considered to be co-tortfeasors under statutes calling for contribution among tortfeasors. See *Foote v. United States* (N.D.Ill. 1986).

What happens when two or more tortfeasors act together to cause a single harm? In most jurisdictions each of the individual tortfeasors is liable to the plaintiff for the entire harm. The liability is considered to be both "joint" (both are liable together) and "several" (each are liable for the entire judgment individually). This enables the plaintiff to recover from either tortfeasor, or both tortfeasors for the entire amount, except that the plaintiff is only entitled to recover until he or she has been fully compensated. No double recoveries are permitted. This is because once the plaintiff's judgment has been satisfied in full from one tortfeasor, that tortfeasor is entitled to seek contribution from the other, usually in the amount of one-half (assuming two tortfeasors) of the judgment. In the few jurisdictions that do not recognize joint and several liability, usually the court will apportion the defendants' liability according to their relative fault, and thereafter the plaintiff must recover from each only what the court has apportioned. Apportionment may also be available in those jurisdiction that do impose joint and several liability, but one or more defendants are able to carry the burden of reasonably apportioning the damages attributable to each defendant.

D. LOSS OF A CHANCE

Another difficult situation occurs when more than one influence comes together to contribute to a plaintiff's injury. One possibility is that the plaintiff in some way contributed to his own condition, for example, by neglecting to follow the physician's instructions. Another possibility is that the plaintiff had a "preexisting condition," i.e. a medical condition that occurred or existed prior to the acts of the defendant which affected the outcome of the plaintiff in a significant way. In the event that there is a preexisting condition, the next inquiry is whether it affected the outcome of the physician's treatment, including negligent treatment. For example, a plaintiff has an inoperable and thus terminal cancer, and is administered a drug to which he is allergic for an unrelated condition. The patient dies of the allergic reaction. The terminal cancer is not relevant to the defendant's liability for the wrongful death, even though the value of the plaintiff's life might be diminished by its quality and life expectancy. In other cases, of course, the preexisting condition is directly related to the treatment which is negligently administered.

The liability of the defendant for the harm caused to a plaintiff with a preexisting condition depends upon how his negligence contributes to the plaintiff's harm. If the negligence results in the worsening of the condition or in the exacerbation of harmful consequences, he is likely to be liable for the increased harm, but not for the preexisting condition.   On the other hand, if the negligence of the physician results in the loss of a possible opportunity for recovery or survival, courts differ on when "loss of a chance" becomes a compensable injury. If, for example, the plaintiff had a small chance of recovery from a certain condition, and the negligence of the defendant deprived the plaintiff of that chance, the question of whether that chance supports a compensable loss is not addressed uniformly by the courts.

In *Boody v. United States* (D.Kan.1989) the plaintiff died after a tumor on her lung, which the defendant failed to diagnose, metastasized and spread to her brain.   There was expert testimony that had the tumor been diagnosed in its early stage, there was a 51% chance that she would have lived for five years; after the metastasis, there was a very slight chance for survival.   Consistent with a growing trend, the federal court specifically rejected the idea that a plaintiff can recover for a loss-of-a-chance only if the probability of a favorable outcome was greater than fifty per cent.   Rather, the court adopted what is now a majority rule that loss-of-a-chance means loss of an "appreciable" chance which depends upon the circumstances of the case. In *Boody*, a 51% chance of surviving for five years was considered an "appreciable" chance.   See also *Herskovits v. Group Health Cooperative of Puget Sound* (Wash.1983) in which the court held that evidence of a reduction in the chance of survival from 39% to 25% was sufficient to go to the jury on the issue of proximate cause. But cf. *Cooper v. Sisters of Charity of Cinn., Inc.* (Ohio 1971) in which the court held that the burden on the plaintiff was to establish that the negligence of the defendant probably caused the death, thus requiring a greater than 50% probability of survival but for the negligence.

Once a court finds that the loss-of-a-chance of survival is a compensable injury, the next inquiry concerns how to value that chance. While there continues to be controversy in this area, the most reasoned approach would appear to restore to the plaintiff that which was lost: the likelihood of having survived multiplied by the value of what was lost. Thus if the chance of survival that was lost due to the negligence of the defendant was 40% that the plaintiff would have lived for five years, the plaintiff should presumably recover 40% of the value of five years of life. In so doing, damages are apportioned directly in relation to the harm that has been caused. More importantly, it eliminates the inequity of depriving plaintiffs of any compensation for the loss-of-chance when they are unable to establish with any certainty that their chance of survival in the absence of the defendant's negligence was at least 50 per cent.

E.   ESTABLISHING PROXIMATE CAUSE

In most medical malpractice actions the burden of proof rests with the plaintiff who must establish by a preponderance of the evidence that the defendant's act was the cause of the harm suffered. The "preponderance of the evidence" standard is the lowest one used in civil actions; it means only that it is "more likely than not" that the plaintiff should prevail. It is also sometimes called the "51%" standard. In essence, it reflects the inherent uncertainty of jury verdicts, and the fact that they are issued upon probabilities that fault really existed. In reconstructing factual situations it often is not possible to be certain about what happened or why, but only to speculate and assign a probability to it being accurate. If the probability is greater than 50%, it is more probable than not.

In the great majority of medical malpractice cases the element of causation must be proved by expert testimony. Since most medical occurrences are not within the common knowledge of the lay jury, expert testimony enables the jury to understand the standard of care, any departures from that standard along with causation and damages. Of course, it requires the jury to make some judgments about the credibility of the expert witnesses and the evidence that they rely upon, but without their assistance the lay jury could do no more than speculate about matters far beyond their possible comprehension.

There are several possible exceptions to the need for expert testimony which have been discussed in depth in Chapter 2. These include situations in which the act or occurrence, as well as its causative effects, are within the general knowledge of the lay jury. They also include situations in which the defendant, through his own testimony, admissions and other evidence is able to provide the necessary expert analysis. Sometimes they include circumstances in which a defendant, having violated a pertinent statute or ordinance, might be presumed to have been negligent. And finally, they may include those situations in which the plaintiff has no knowledge of how or what caused his injury, but the injury is such that it usually does not occur in the absence of negligence. With the aid of res ipsa loquitur, the plaintiff may be able to secure a permissible inference of negligence, sufficient to get to the jury which is entitled, but not required, to return a judgment for the plaintiff. For a discussion of these exceptions, see Chapter 2.

Because of the difficulty in making a definitive determination about whether a certain act proximately caused the plaintiff's injury, experts are usually asked to give their opinion about the probability that a certain medical event caused a certain outcome. Once again the question arises about exactly how certain they must be to make a judgment, and how the jury should evaluate a less-than-certain opinion. The traditional rule is that an expert is expected to state only those opinions which he is sure about "to a reasonable degree of medical certainty." The difficulty comes in deciding what this phrase means and how strictly the element of "reasonableness" should be interpreted. For example, one approach is to require that the direct and circumstantial evidence in the case (e.g., understanding of the particular subject matter, availability of requisite medical history and facts about the occurrence) allow the expert to form an opinion about the occurrence "to a reasonable degree of medical certainty." The alternative approach is to view the reasonable-degree-of-medical certainty as tantamount to carrying the ultimate burden of proof. Thus, the reasonable degree refers to whether it is "more likely than not" that the injury to the plaintiff was proximately caused by the negligence of the defendant. The second approach demonstrates the critical importance of expert testimony.

Medical malpractice cases often stand or fall on the opinions of the experts and the credibility assigned to their testimony. Some courts, however, reject the implicit conclusion of expert's testimony as being tantamount to a legal determination of proximate cause. Thus some trial courts will prevent the experts from purporting to testify as to the "ultimate issue" in a case, i.e., the determination of proximate cause. Such courts view proximate cause as a legal issue based upon a determination of all of the elements of the case: a duty of care, a breach of that duty, causation and damages. The role of the expert is to provide his medical opinion, but not to apply the law to the particular facts of the case. These courts may be troubled by the possibility that the jury would give undue weight to the ultimate conclusion of an expert who is willing to offer one. Other courts are willing to give limiting instructions to the jury which remind it that the opinions of the experts are just that: opinions, and it is the jury that ultimately makes the determination of liability.

II. DAMAGES

The final requisite element in proving a cause of action for medical malpractice is the determination that the plaintiff suffered a compensable harm as a result of the defendant's wrongful act. Two types of damages are potentially available. Compensatory damages are intended to compensate the plaintiff for the actual harm suffered, including the pain and suffering of the plaintiff. Punitive damages are available in certain types of cases and are intended to punish a defendant who wilfully or recklessly causes harm to a plaintiff. Restatement (Second) of Torts § 908(2)

The dollar amount that is available in medical malpractice cases is governed, in large part, by the rules of personal injury practice of the jurisdiction. Plaintiffs who sustain their burden of proof for tort claims can recover out-of-pocket losses (medical bills and future medical expense), loss of income and impairment of earning capacity, incidental expenses, and recovery of an amount that represents the pain, suffering and mental distress of the injured plaintiff. Plaintiffs who prove claims based upon breach of contract because a practitioner promised a particular result or otherwise made a contractual promise may be entitled to a contract measure of damages based upon the value of the expectancy, the detrimental reliance caused by a promise, or an unjust enrichment of the defendant. See, generally, Chapter 9 for a discussion of contract remedies. Punitive (or "exemplary") damages are generally measured on the basis of what it takes to "punish" a grossly negligent, wilful or reckless tortfeasor, and a jury determination on that issue is often unpredictable. In some jurisdictions, punitive damages are expected to bear a relationship to the compensable damages, but in others substantial discretion is permitted.

III. SPECIFIC TYPES OF DAMAGE AWARDS

A. WRONGFUL LIFE AND WRONGFUL BIRTH

Claims for "wrongful life" or "wrongful birth" are typically brought when a physician negligently fails to advise expectant parents that their child may be handicapped, or otherwise fails to act so that expectant parents can make an informed choice about whether to proceed with a pregnancy. Wrongful birth usually refers to a claim made by the parents of a handicapped child on the basis of the emotional distress and medical expenses to them; wrongful life is often a companion claim brought by the child who claims that but for the physician's negligence, he or she would not be impaired, or would not have been born at all. In yet other cases, (sometimes called "wrongful pregnancy" or "wrongful conception") a normal and healthy child is born, but one that was unintended and occurred as a result of negligence (e.g. negligent performance of a sterilization procedure.) In each case the question arises as to what, if any, damages are available to compensate the disappointed parents.

Damages for claims of wrongful life and wrongful birth and sometimes wrongful conception are not assessed uniformly among the jurisdictions. In a growing number of cases for wrongful birth, courts have been willing to allow the jury to assess damages based upon the cost of the impairment to the lives of the parents, including extraordinary medical bills, disruptions to the family and emotional distress caused by the handicap. This presumes, of course, that the plaintiff is able to sustain the burden of proof that there was negligence on the part of the practitioner in failing to perform certain diagnostic tests or otherwise detect a physical or genetic abnormality. It also presumes that the negligence results in the child's impairment or the parents' inability to opt to terminate the pregnancy.

In a case brought by the child for wrongful life, courts may be willing to compensate the child for expenses associated with the handicap, and even for the pain and suffering that the child must endure. However, a majority of courts are unwilling to provide redress for the claim that a child's life of impairment makes him worse off than if he had never been born at all. Thus in those cases where the claim is that but for the physician's negligence the child would have been aborted, most courts are unwilling to engage in the difficult task of trying to compare the value of an impaired life to that of no life at all. Often (but not always) the result is that no damages are awarded for the "wrongful life." See *Lininger v. Eisenbaum* (Colo.1988). A few courts that have held to the contrary include some in California, Washington and New Jersey. See, e.g. *Procanik v. Cillo* (N.J.1984).

Probably the most difficult actions for calculating damages are those involving wrongful conception. When a normal and healthy child is born, courts differ in their approach to assessing damages against a negligent physician who, for example, failed to properly perform the sterilization procedure. A majority of such courts will award medical expenses that result from the physician's negligence (including another sterilization), compensation for the parents' physical and mental pain and suffering and other consequential damages such as loss of wages. Occasionally punitive damages are available. On the other hand, ordinary child rearing expenses incurred as a result of the negligence are generally not recoverable, and many courts reach this conclusion by offsetting the amount recoverable by the parents by the so-called "benefits rule". This measures the benefit to most parents of having a healthy child in both pecuniary and non-pecuniary terms. See *C.S. v. Nielson* (Utah 1988).

B. DIGNITARY TORTS

Another area in which in has traditionally been difficult to measure damages is the so-called "torts of dignity.'' For example, in *Berthiaume's Estate v. Pratt* (Me.1976) a dying patient clearly indicated through hand and facial gestures that he objected to the taking of photographs of him which had no therapeutic function. The pictures were taken despite his objection. The court was willing to recognize potential liability of the hospital for invasion of the patient's right of privacy.

In another case, *Strachan v. John F. Kennedy Mem. Hosp.* (N.J.1988), the parents of a brain-dead 20–year-old were asked to consider donation of their son's organs. When they refused the hospital allegedly delayed disconnecting the life support system, hoping that the parents might be convinced to change their minds. It ultimately took three days between the determination of brain death and the termination of life support. In the parents' action against the hospital for negligent handling of a corpse and prevention of a proper burial the trial court awarded $140,000 for the mental suffering occasioned by tortious conduct.

The rules concerning dignitary torts vary widely among jurisdictions, as do the damages that might be awarded in such a case. Unlike typical negligence cases, however, a cause of action will generally lie for the harm caused, even if there is no physical injury. Generally claims against dignity are intentional actions, and the damages that are recoverable reflect the emotional distress and suffering of the plaintiff.

C. HARM TO ONESELF

With increasing frequency claims are being waged against health care professionals for the self-inflicted injuries of patients who prove to be a danger to themselves. Physicians who regularly attend psychiatric patients are often required to choose between involuntarily confining those who may pose a danger to themselves and permitting their freedom, with the risk of possible harm. Commitment decisions are made on the basis of the available information. A physician is not negligent merely because his judgment yields a bad result. If, on the other hand, he acts in way that is contrary to the applicable standard of due care, an action against him may be founded. In *Widgeon v. Eastern Shore Hospital Center* (Md.1984), supra, a man was involuntarily committed to a psychiatric facility on the basis of a false tale told by his wife. When he was brought in for examination, he demonstrated no "outward" signs of mental illness, but was confined anyway. The court held that a cause of action had been stated.

The potential for liability also exists, however, when a physician declines to confine a dangerous person who later inflicts injury on himself. The same standards of due care and negligence apply. A physician who acts unreasonably and in so doing fails to prevent a suicide or other self-destructive behavior may be liable for the natural consequences of his lack of due care. The difficulty that these cases present is in the question of whether there is proximate cause between the negligence and the self-destructive acts. It has been argued that those acts constitute a superseding cause that should defeat liability. On the other hand, presumably there is no negligence unless it was reasonably foreseeable that self-inflicted injury was a danger. If that is, in fact, the case, failure to prevent the injury should be actionable. The considered approach is to separate the issues of due care and proximate cause from those of cause-in-fact, since the cause-in-fact will usually be the patient's own actions.

D. PUNITIVE OR EXEMPLARY DAMAGES

The traditional rules governing personal injury actions for calculation of damages are equally applicable in the medical malpractice context. Thus in addition to recovery for pecuniary losses, pain and suffering and emotional distress, there exists the possibility that a plaintiff may be entitled to punitive or exemplary damages. Such damages are considered when "... the act or omission complained of was the result of a conscious indifference to the right or welfare of the ... persons affected by it." *McPhearson v. Sullivan* (Tex.1971). The conduct must be more than merely negligent; it must be egregious or it must result from the wilful, wanton or reckless conduct of the practitioner.

In *Jackson v. Taylor* (5th Cir.1990) the plaintiff suffered from bleeding liver tumors as a result of birth control pills prescribed by the defendant. Expert testimony was presented concerning the defendant's standard of care which was described to be grossly negligent. In particular, the record contained unrebutted information that the plaintiff had purchased over 1000 pills within a period that less than 200 were appropriate. The appellate court held that if the pleadings and evidence raise the issue of gross negligence, the court must submit a special interrogatory to the jury on the issue of exemplary damages. Like all other elements of the plaintiff's case, gross negligence is generally proved on the basis of expert testimony which describes the extent of the breach of the applicable standard of due care.

IV. DAMAGE AWARDS AND MALPRACTICE REFORM

The law of medical malpractice has become an ever-expanding field with the theories of liability and the number of cases rising dramatically. Serious attention in recent years has been given to reform of the system, primarily to bring down the high cost of health care which is due, in some measure, to the costs of practicing medicine. Malpractice reform will be discussed in greater detail in Chapter 10, but some reforms, notably those that impact directly on damage awards, are already in place. These include statutory ceilings on the amount of damages that can be awarded in a particular care, as well as limitations on the contingent fees that lawyers can collect for extraordinary verdicts. Constitutional challenges have been raised in some states concerning damage limitations. Regardless of the mechanism of reform, state have not been uniform in the resolution of the issues.

One of the most common limitations is a statutory cap on the amount of damages that can be awarded in a malpractice case. In some states such damage limitations have been held constitutional, as a legitimate means of furthering an important state interest i.e., addressing the medical malpractice crisis which is responsible, in part, for the exorbitant costs of health care. See, e.g., West's Ann. Ind. Code 16–9.5–2–2 (1984). In others, however, the distinction between medical malpractice actions and other personal injury suits has led courts to hold such limitations to be unconstitutional as a violation of the equal protection of the laws. See Vernon's Ann.Tex.Civ. Stat. arts. 4590, 5511.02, 11.04 (Supp. 1985).

Another avenue of reform of medical malpractice litigation that has been considered concerns the availability of additional compensation to a plaintiff from collateral sources. In general, the rule is that a plaintiff who is able to protect himself from possible loss by carrying insurance or receiving compensation from other "collateral" sources has no obligation to reduce the obligation of a wrongdoer by the amount received from a collateral source. As between an innocent plaintiff and a culpable wrongdoer, the plaintiff yields the benefit of the collateral source. Some states have attempted to abrogate the common law rule in cases of medical malpractice (specifically insurance payments) in order to reduce the overall damage awards. Once again, some states, but not others, have found the abrogation of the common law to be constitutional. See *Fein v. Permanente Medical Group* (Cal.1985) (holding such a statute constitutional.) See also *Doran v. Priddy* (D.Kan.1981).

The medical malpractice "crisis" which formally took hold in the mid–1970's reaches greater and greater proportions each year. As a result, many of the proposed reforms of health care have focused on reforming the litigation system and limiting the damages that can be awarded for medical injuries. See Chapter 10. Many proposals exists, from creating a "no-fault" system for medical accidents to overhauling the jury system to further limiting the amount of recovery available to victims. In each case the challenge is to balance a fair system of compensation for victims with one that provides an incentive for a high standard of medical care.

CHAPTER SIX

AFFIRMATIVE DEFENSES, LIMITATIONS AND IMMUNITIES

I. IN GENERAL: STATUTES OF LIMITATIONS

Statutes of limitations are generally enacted to limit the amount of time in which a plaintiff can bring a cause of action against an alleged wrong-doer. The goal of these statutes is to balance the needs of the plaintiff to have a reasonable period of time to bring an action with those of the defendant who would otherwise be subject to potential liability for an indefinite period of time. Additionally, the statutes serve to avoid overburdening the judicial system with stale claims that are difficult to establish because evidence may be lost and the memories of credible witnesses fade. A number of states have a separate statute of limitations for medical malpractice actions. A court's decision as to whether a particular malpractice action is brought within the applicable limitations period depends upon the length of the period as defined by the statute, and any factors that might serve to toll the running of the limitations period. See Nancy E. Leibowitz, Statute of Limitations—Medical Malpractice—Constitutional Law—Five Year Statute of Repose on Medical Malpractice Claims That Commences When An Injury Occurs is Constitutional, 16 U. Balt. L. Rev. 571 (1987).

A. STANDARD RULES FOR ACCRUAL OF ACTIONS

The standard rule is that the statutory period of limitation commences at the point in time at which the cause of action "accrues". Accrual is defined by statute and is generally said to occur when the allegedly negligent act occurs, or when it results in damage. For example, some jurisdictions specify the date of the alleged occurrence, holding that the cause of action accrues on the date of the alleged malpractice act. See *Payton v. Benson* (S.D.Ind. 1989). Other jurisdictions have held that an action accrues when actual damage results, or on the date of "injury" if the statute is so phrased. In *Mastro v. Brodie* (Colo.1984), the Colorado Supreme Court held that even the word "injury" is subject to different interpretations. For example, it can refer to the negligent act or omission, or to the actual physical damage that results or to the alleged injury.

Statutes of limitations may also be modified by other legislation, particularly that which is enacted specifically to address the particular concerns associated with the medical malpractice crisis. For example, in Indiana, the two year statute of limitations is "tolled" by the filing of a timely complaint with the Department of Insurance which reviews such cases and produces a written opinion. Pursuant to that legislative tolling provision, the plaintiff has a minimum of 90 days after the decision of the medical panel to file suit, and longer if the two year statute of limitations has not yet expired.

Statutes which are interpreted as defining accrual from the time of the act or omission may raise certain constitutional issues. In *Chaffin v. Nicosia* (Ind.1974), the plaintiff allegedly lost an eye at birth as a result of the use of forceps during delivery and brought suit when he was 22 years old. In ruling on the statute of limitations issue, the court was forced to reconcile two statutes with seemingly inconsistent provisions. The statute applicable to malpractice actions required the plaintiff to bring suit within two years of the alleged incident. A second statute, applicable to lawsuits brought on behalf of the minors, allowed suit to be brought up to two years after the plaintiff attained majority. The plaintiff contended that his cause of action was not barred by the malpractice statute of limitations, but was protected by the statute which recognized the legal disability of a minor for bringing suit. Under this law, the suit was timely since it was filed less two years after the time the plaintiff reached the age of 21 years. The lower courts held the suit barred by the state's two-year malpractice statute. The Supreme Court reversed, holding that to bar such a claim would offend the constitution and the legislature's intent in making the disability exception. As stated by the court, "[t]o construe [the] medical malpractice statute, which bars all suits which are not brought within two years of the occurrence of which complaint is made, as a legislative bar in all malpractice actions under all circumstances unless commenced within two years of the act complained of, discoverable or otherwise, would raise substantial questions under constitutional article relating to the guarantee of open courts and redress for injury to every man, not to mention the offense to lay concepts of justice."

Statutes of limitations, while seemingly rigid, have been subject to varying interpretations, as well as a major exception found primarily in medical malpractice actions: the discovery rule.

B. DISCOVERY RULES:
PURE AND HYBRID

In medical malpractice cases, where expert opinion is often needed to determine that malpractice has indeed occurred, it often happens that an injured plaintiff is unaware that he has suffered an injury, particularly if the injury is latent or internal. An injured patient may also not be able to associate the injury with an act or omission of the medical professional. Yet, these determinations must be made in a timely manner in order to file a claim within the traditional statute of limitations. In recognition of the reality that some medical injuries are inherently unknowable during the applicable statute of limitations, virtually all jurisdictions have carved out exceptions to the standard rule, or have redefined the statute to encompass what is known as the "discovery rule". The "discovery rule" generally provides that a cause of action must be brought within a specified period of time from the date that the injury is discovered, or, in the exercise of reasonable diligence, should have been discovered. See *Burns v. Hartford Hospital* (Conn.1984) (Act specifies discovery rule); *Doyle v. Shubs* (D.Mass.1989) (defining accrual by time of discovery of injury). Pure discovery rules will allow a claim to be brought for an indefinite period of time as long as the injury has not been discovered or reasonably should not have been discovered.

An alternative or "hybrid" version of the discovery rule is also followed in some states. According to the hybrid version, discovery of the injury triggers the running of the statute of limitation, but an ultimate cap or limit is placed upon the time within which discovery must occur. For example, a statute may require that an action be commenced within two years of discovery of the injury, but also contains an additional provision that requires the filing of the action within three years of the act or omission. The latter provision is called a "statute of repose." In such a case, the claimant has at least two years to file the claim, and no more than three, depending upon when and if the injury is discovered. See *Mastro v. Brodie* (Colo.1984).

Many jurisdictions have expressly interpreted the discovery rule to apply only to situations where the injury is inherently unknowable, or to malpractice actions where a foreign body, such as a sponge, had been left in a wound during surgery. See *Cloutier v. Dalkon Shield Claimants Trust* (D.Maine 1993). In a move to expand the rule, one court stated,

"a steadily growing and now predominant line of decisions in other states which recognize the discovery rule, as such, acknowledges there is no just basis for distinguishing between different kinds of malpractice claims in applying the discovery rule, since, in all, the basic hardship and injustice of denying an injured plaintiff his day in court remains."

Moran v. Napolitano (N.J.1976). According to this line of reasoning, the discovery rule can be applied in all types of malpractice actions, including error in diagnosis.

It is important to note that reliance upon a physician's assurance that an injury is not permanent may not be effective in tolling the applicable statute of limitations. In *Burns v. Hartford Hospital* (Conn.1984), a child's leg was permanently injured from an infection resulting from contaminated intravenous tubes which were placed in the leg by the hospital staff. The doctor had assured the mother that the leg would heal completely, but the child suffered damage from scarring and an abnormality in his gait. The court held that "the act of this intervening third party, who may have misled the plaintiff about the injury's seriousness or even compounded the harm by failing to render effective treatment, cannot extend the hospital's liability be-

yond the statutory limitation period." The court
implied, however, that there may have been a different result if the doctor had been alleged to be the
agent of the hospital.

The discovery rule may also generate some confusion as to when discovery of "the injury" occurs
since what constitutes the "injury" may have varying interpretations. According to Mastro, a majority of states have adopted a "legal injury" interpretation of the word "injury". Under that concept,
"the statute of limitations begins to run when the
claimant has knowledge of facts which would put a
reasonable person on notice of the nature and extent of an injury and that the injury was caused by
the wrongful conduct of another." *Mastro*. It
seems that lack of either knowledge of the injury or
its possible cause would enable a plaintiff to take
advantage of the discovery rule.

The question of when a patient, through the
exercise of due diligence, should reasonably have
discovered an injury is also the subject of frequent
litigation. For example, in *Mastro*, a woman developed a discomforting keloid scar following surgery.
She returned to the surgeon who provided some
care and reassurance. Finally, more than two years
after the surgery, the patient visited a specialist
who advised her of her high risk status for keloid
scarring. One issue was whether she should have
known or diligently discovered that the surgery was
performed negligently. Another issue was whether
the doctor failed to obtain proper informed consent
as he had not informed her of her high risk status.

The patient argued that discovery occurred upon her consultation with a specialist. The court held that the determination of the point of discovery was a fact question for the jury and denied summary judgment.

C. THE CONTINUING TREATMENT RULE AND FRAUDULENT CONCEALMENT

Another issue that arises in determining the time of injury for statute of limitations purposes is that treatment sometimes continues for a period of time and it can be difficult to ascertain when the negligence occurred. A number of jurisdictions have adopted a "continuing treatment" rule to address the issue. Pursuant to this doctrine, accrual of the cause of action may be postponed if there is continued treatment of the patient by the allegedly negligent physician for the particular condition that is the subject of the complaint. This rule provides an exception to the usual inflexible application of the statute of limitations and may extend the time allowed for the filing of a complaint. According to the continuing treatment rule, the cause of action would only accrue when treatment of the condition ceases. Cessation of treatment can be determined on the basis of whether a physician-patient relationship continues to exist, whether the physician continues to see the patient or whether there is additional treatment for the same condition still to be done by the physician. See *Noland v. Freeman* (Minn.1984). Whether on-going treatment qualifies under the continuing treatment rule is a question or fact for the jury.

Finally, sometimes statutes of limitations will also be tolled if the physician is found to have "knowingly concealed" the negligent act or omission. If knowing concealment is found, a plaintiff has the statutory period of time to file the complaint which begins when he "should have known" about the negligent act or omission. See *Mastro*. The rules for fraudulent concealment have evolved through recognition of the fiduciary nature of the physician-patient relationship, which would require the physician to disclose to the patient information which is material to his treatment. This doctrine is considered to be a form of equitable estoppel rather that an exception to the rules concerning statutes of limitations.

D. REFORMS

The above mechanisms for tolling the statutes of limitations have evolved primarily as a result of the complexities of medical practice that may make it unfair to impose the rigid requirements of the traditional statutes of limitations. As a result a number of jurisdictions have also undertaken to reform such statutes, while recognizing the need for imposing a limitations period. Reform of an individual statute depends upon the purpose of the statute (whether it is thought to protect primarily plaintiffs or defendants) and whether the goal is to reduce the costs of malpractice. Often the period in which a medical malpractice claim can be brought depends upon when the claim is said to "accrue" or discovery is said to occur. A number of reform measures have been initiated to provide clarification of how these events are determined including the factors to be considered. The goal is to provide more predictability for defendants and their insurers, who not only defend such cases, but also set rates for insurance coverage. Statutes of repose, for example, have been enacted in recent years to limit the uncertainty generated by the discovery rule.

II. GOOD SAMARITAN LAWS

Good Samaritan Laws have been enacted in most jurisdictions to induce physicians to render emergency care under circumstances in which they have no legal obligation to act. This includes medical emergencies that occur in areas outside of the health care setting, (e.g. on the street, in a restaurant, etc.) or inside a health care facility at a time or place that the responsible physician is not available. A physician who happens to be present or readily available can usually act in such an emergency without incurring liability even if he is negligent. Prior to enactment of Good Samaritan legislation, the common law provided a remedy by reducing the standard of care that would be used in evaluating the quality of treatment. This, however, did not discourage the initiation of malpractice actions. The Good Samaritan laws, first enacted in California, were designed to alter the common law by providing added protection for those offering services in emergency situations. Today, many laws specify guidelines where claims of ordinary negligence may be dismissed before reaching the jury. See *Colby v. Schwartz* (Cal.App.1978).

The first issue in determining whether a physician or other health care provider is covered under a particular Good Samaritan law is whether the law was intended to reach his actions under the specific circumstances. For example, the law does not apply to a physician who renders care in the normal course of his practice, such as when he is a member of an emergency room team. On the other hand, the Good Samaritan laws have been held to apply in certain other hospital emergency situations. In *McKenna v. Cedars of Lebanon Hospital* (Cal.App. 1979), where a chief resident responded to an emergency situation involving a hospital patient having post-operative seizures, the court held he was protected by the Good Samaritan law. According to *McKenna*, the applicability of the law depends on whether the doctor had a duty to respond. In that case, the hospital patient was not the resident's patient, nor did his contract with the hospital require him to respond to emergencies.

The applicability of Good Samaritan laws varies among jurisdictions. A contrary result would be reached in a jurisdiction which precludes the application of the Good Samaritan laws in the hospital setting. For example, some statutes specify that the emergency must occur outside the physician's normal place of practice. See *McKenna*. Other statutes may apply not only to physicians, but also to nurses and certain other personnel such as emergency medical technicians (EMT's) who render aid during the emergency situation. See *Tatum v. Gigliotti* (Md.1991).

Other limitations which affect the application of the law depend upon specific provisions of the statute. In *Villamil v. Benages* (Ill.App.1993), the statute set forth a three-part test: (1) The care must be provided by a physician with no notice of the illness or injury; (2) emergency care must be provided; and (3) the physician must not charge a fee. These conditions can be satisfied in the hospital setting as well as in a roadside emergency. In *Villamil*, a physician was present in the hospital attending another patient, and was called to assist in the delivery of a premature baby. The patient came into the emergency room. She did not have time to reach the hospital of her choice. On summary judgment, the physician was held to be protected by the Illinois Good Samaritan law. *Villamil*.

Other jurisdictions provide that a physician or other health professional is protected if he acts *in good faith* to render emergency care. The issue of whether the situation constitutes an emergency is sometimes resolved by an objective test, such as whether the circumstances are so pressing as to require some action to be taken. On the other hand, the requirement that there be a "good faith" belief on the part of the responding physician that an emergency exists may be a subjective determination. As a result, it may be difficult to dispose of these cases by summary judgment. *Bryant v. Bak-shandeh* (Cal.App.1991).

In Bryant, an infant boy was being prepared for elective surgery requiring insertion of a urethral catheter. The attending physician had difficulty inserting the catheter and called for the assistance of a urologist. The child later died from an infection resulting from the perforation of his rectal pouch during this preoperative procedure. A question of fact existed as to the nature of the situation and whether "in good faith" it could be perceived as an emergency. The surgeon characterized the situation as an "unforeseen complexity" which the court held was not determinative. Summary judgment was thus denied.

The varying forms of Good Samaritan legislation represent the efforts of each jurisdiction to balance two competing interests: compensating those injured through medical negligence and encouraging physicians and other health professionals to provide emergency medical care under circumstances where there is no particular compulsion to do so. The latter interest is promoted by Good Samaritan legislation. See *Colby v. Schwartz*.

III. OTHER AFFIRMATIVE DEFENSES
A. CONTRIBUTORY NEGLIGENCE

The traditional doctrine of contributory negligence requires that a plaintiff be free of any fault or negligence which may contribute to the severity of his injury in order to recover damages. In some jurisdictions, contributory negligence operates as a total bar to recovery. In such cases, a plaintiff who contributes to his own injury is precluded from recovering for his injuries from the tortfeasor. See *Schneider v. Revici* (2d Cir.1987). The doctrine is said to operate as a defense to an action where "a party knows or by the exercise of ordinary care should have known a particular fact or circumstance and should have acted upon the fact or circumstance with reasonable care for his own safety." *Weil v. Seltzer* (D.C.Cir.1989) In the context of medical malpractice, a patient is not ordinarily expected to know that a prescribed treatment or procedure was performed negligently, or that there were undisclosed risks that may have influenced his decision to undergo the procedure. Such medical decisions often require the expertise of the physician. As a consequence, contributory negligence is generally not available to mitigate a physician's negligence if the patient was merely following the orders of the physician. *Weil v. Seltzer*.

Similarly, a patient is not necessarily contributorily negligent if he seeks consultation from another doctor during the course of treatment, and thereafter refuses to follow the consulting physician's advise. Here, the original physician-patient relationship was not terminated, and the patient does not contribute to his own injury in following the advise of the treating physician. See *Weinstock v. Ott* (Ind.App.1983). In *Ott*, a woman, suffering from abdominal pain for almost two years, was under the care of a physician when she sought the advice of a second physician. She had already undergone multiple tests during two hospitalizations. The consulting physician recommended more tests, although he was not able to provide the patient with any other diagnosis at that point. The woman declined to undergo the additional testing but continued to see her original physician. In fact, she checked herself out of the second hospital, after many tests failed to provide any explanation or yield any improvement of her condition. Nearly four years later, the condition was finally correctly diagnosed at the second hospital. Nevertheless, the patient eventually died of complications brought about by the advanced stage of the disease. The court held that she was not contributorily negligent as a matter of law in failing to follow the advise of the consultant or by checking herself out of the second hospital. She had been provided with no further information, and thus opted to continue to see and follow the advise of her original physician for the entire period of time.

B. COMPARATIVE NEGLIGENCE

An alternative to the all-or-nothing consequence of contributory negligence is the principles of comparative negligence, and many jurisdictions have adopted one form or another. In general, the theory of comparative negligence is that any negligence on the part of the plaintiff is "compared" to that of the tortfeasor, and that any damages ultimately awarded to the plaintiff are reduced by the percentage of negligence attributed to the plaintiff.

There are three possible forms of comparative negligence adopted in various jurisdictions. The first is "pure" comparative negligence. In such a case a plaintiff, regardless of how much his own negligence contributes to his injury, will still be able to recover something from a negligent tortfeasor. The percentage of negligence attributed to his conduct is deducted in the same percentage from the dollar amount of the total award. See *Shelton v. United States* (E.D.Mo.1992). The remaining forms of comparative negligence permit recovery of a contributory negligent plaintiff to be reduced by the percentage attributed to his own negligence, but only if the plaintiff's contribution is less that 50 percent of the total negligence or, in other states, less than 51 percent of the total negligence.

Comparative negligence attempts to apportion fault and damages based on the relative contribution to the injury by all the parties involved. The respective contributions toward causation may be compared and the damages due to the patient may be reduced in proportion to the fault of the patient. In *Shelton*, the court held the physician was negligent in not prescribing antibiotics for a bite wound. However, the patient's negligence in not following discharge instructions and returning promptly for medical care when the infection was observed was held to constitute a 50 percent contribution to the injury, resulting in subsequent amputation of the finger. Therefore, the plaintiff's award of damages was reduced by 50 percent.

C. AVOIDABLE CONSEQUENCES
AND LAST CLEAR CHANCE

The theory of comparative negligence is often used to apportion damage when the related doctrines of "avoidable consequences" or "last clear chance" are set forth. Each is based upon the assumption that in some cases a plaintiff, while not responsible for his injury, had some opportunity to avoid or mitigate the results. These doctrines operate after the legal wrong has caused the harm. The theory is that the patient should not recover for what he could have avoided or mitigated, although recovery need not be totally barred. Contributory negligence, in contrast, operates before or concurrently with the medical malpractice and may bar a plaintiff's recovery. See *Ostrowski v. Azzara* (N.J. 1988).

Comparative negligence may also still be applied even in situations where the injured plaintiff has relocated to another jurisdiction and continued care in that location. For example, a federal court in New Jersey held that such relocation did not prevent the allocation of causative fault between the non-settling physicians and the settling physician in another jurisdiction, since the claims were found to be identical and interwoven. See *Carter v. University of Medicine and Dentistry of New Jersey— Rutgers Medical School* (D.N.J.1994). Conflict of laws rules may also affect the application of law when a plaintiff moves to another jurisdiction.

D. PRIOR AND SUBSEQUENT TORTFEASORS

A doctor who participates in a physician-patient relationship and thereby incurs a duty to a patient may also be held liable for injuries caused by a subsequent physician, if such physician attempts to remedy a condition caused by him. See *Daly v. United States* (9th Cir.1991). Thus a physician who causes injury may be held liable for subsequent aggravation of that injury even if it occurs through additional medical malpractice. See *Moller v. North Shore University Hospital* (E.D.N.Y.1992); *Tyler v. Ahmed* (11th Cir.1987).

Many states have adopted some form of the Uniform Contribution Among Tortfeasors Act which would provide a right of contribution among joint tortfeasors. Ordinarily a joint tortfeasor is not entitled to receive money from contributing tortfeasors unless he has fully paid the common liability or paid more that his pro rata share. See Fed. R. Civ. P., Rule 14 Annotations; *Smith v. Whitmore* (3d Cir.1959); *Huggins v. Graves* (E.D.Tenn. 1962); Penn. Uniform Contribution Among Joint Tortfeasors Act, 12 P.S. sec. 2083.

E. ASSUMPTION OF THE RISK

Assumption of the risk is a legal doctrine which is based upon the premise that some products or procedures contain inherent risks and that when so informed of them, plaintiffs may agree to assume responsibility for an occurrence that might result.

Assumption of the risk, as compared to contributory or comparative negligence, focuses on what the patient actually knew as opposed to what the patient should have known. For example, if a patient knew a particular risk of a medical procedure and nevertheless submitted to it, assumption of the risk may bar recovery for any resulting injuries associated with that known risk, although not for negligence. See *Weil v. Seltzer* (D.C.Cir.1989).

At common law, one cannot assume the risk of another's negligence. Such an action would rarely be sustained, even if an individual does assume the risk of another's negligence. See Exculpatory Clauses, infra. Nevertheless, in *Schneider v. Revici* (2d Cir.1987), the second circuit held that a patient who consented to non-conventional experimental treatment, foregoing traditional methods, might be held to have assumed the risk of any worsening of his condition. In *Schneider* the use of non-traditional therapies would probably constitute an inherent risk, and not necessarily be considered negligence.

Assumption of the risk can either be express (as through a consent form) or implied by the circumstances. In order for a patient to be held to have expressly assume a risk, there must be clear evidence, such as a written consent form. To claim express assumption of the risk as a defense, there must be evidence that the patient had knowledge of the risk, appreciated and understood the nature of the risk, and voluntarily chose to incur it. See *Shorter v. Drury* (Wash.1985). *Shorter* involved a

Jehovah's Witness who executed a written "Refusal to Permit a Blood Transfusion", as well as a release from liability for any untoward results of doing so. The patient was admitted to the hospital for a dilation and curettage procedure and subsequently bled to death after the surgeon negligently lacerated her uterus. The court held that the release did not exculpate the physician from his negligence in lacerating the patient's uterus. It did, however, constitute an acceptance of the risk of refusing blood. The patient bled to death, which would normally have been avoided by the transfusion. The court held that the physician could still be liable for his negligence, although damages were reduced because of the patient's acceptance of the risk.

IV. LIMITATIONS ON LIABILITY
A. RELEASES

At common law, a release of one joint tortfeasor released all tortfeasors from liability. This rule evolved from the principle that a victim was entitled to be compensated only once for his injury in order to avoid unjust enrichment. This rule included concurrent tortfeasors as well as those acting in concert. The common law rule seems to have developed as a result of confusion within some courts about the concepts of "satisfaction" and "release". Satisfaction indicates full compensation for the injury, while a release is a surrender of the cause of action, whether or not it has been satisfied. Many courts hold that a release of one of concurrent tortfeasors releases all the others, without considering whether there has been just or adequate compensation. For example, in *Tyler v. Ahmed* (11th Cir.1987), the court held that a plaintiff who settled a claim with her auto insurance company for all of her injuries cannot thereafter sue the physician who treated her injuries for malpractice. The express settlement of all damages results in the rights of the insured being subrogated to the insurance company. The court also pointed out that the insured knowingly compromised all of her claims as part of the settlement, regardless of whether she actually received full recovery.

The modern view of releases is that, absent clear language to the contrary, a subsequent tortfeasor such as a negligent treating physician is not released from liability as a matter of law. The common law interpretation of releases has also been modified by statute in many jurisdictions. For example, in those who have adopted the Uniform Contribution Among Tortfeasors Act, a tortfeasor would only be released from liability "if the release so provides".

In *Morgan v. Cohen* (Md.1987), a malpractice action was brought against a physician for negligent treatment of injuries that the plaintiff sustained in an auto accident. The claim had been settled with the auto insurance company and the settlement included a general release. In contrast to *Tyler*, *Morgan* held that because Maryland had abrogated the common law rule by adopting the Uniform Contribution Among Tortfeasors Act, the general release did not discharge the physician as a matter of law. The determination of whether the physician was released, was held to depend upon the intent of the parties and whether the satisfaction included all the damages. *Morgan*, supra.

In *Douglas v. U.S. Tobacco Company* (8th Cir. 1982), the eight circuit interpreted the phrase "all other persons" contained in a general release to satisfy the "if the release so provides" condition in the local version of the Uniform Contribution Among Tortfeasors Act. Thus, any subsequent tortfeasor would be discharged from liability regardless of actual compensation that might have been received. This position is followed by a majority of jurisdictions.

Similarly, an Ohio court held that an unconditional release, executed with advise of counsel and for consideration, presumptively released all wrongdoers and barred an action for aggravation of injury. The release specified that losses sustained and *resulting* from the accident were included. See *Whitt v. Hutchison* (Ohio 1975). However, the court also held that, if the presumption is rebutted, subsequent tortfeasors may not be released.

A written release which is silent about its effect on the parties may be interpreted differently. *McCullough v. Bethany Medical Center* (Kan.1984) was such a case, and the court held that the parties were presumed not released. Furthermore, parol evidence was permitted to determine the intention of the parties. Likewise, certain statutory provisions may require that the release expressly release subsequent tortfeasors in order for them to avoid liability. See *Moller v. North Shore University Hospital* (E.D.N.Y.1992). Furthermore, the applicable statute also provided that subsequent claims would be set-off by the amount of damages already received.

B. EXCULPATORY CLAUSES

Occasionally a physician or institution will attempt to make agreements with patients that exempt the health care provider from liability for ordinary negligence. For example, some clinics which train students may attempt to offer services at a reduced price as consideration for absolving themselves of liability. See *Emory University v. Porubiansky* (Ga.1981). Exculpatory clauses in agreements which limit liability for negligence are uniformly held to be unenforceable for purposes of medical malpractice because they are contrary to public policy. See *Tunkl v. Regents of the University of California* (Cal.1963). In *Tunkl*, a charitable research hospital required patients, as a condition of admission, to exculpate the hospital for the negligence of its employees, as long as it used due care in selecting them. The California Civil Code, however, prohibited exculpatory clauses for "violations of law, whether willful or negligent", which affect the public interest. The court did state that the rule against exculpatory clauses may be different in the case of a private transaction which had no effect on the public interest.

In the case of a patient entering a hospital, particularly a charitable research hospital, the public interest is clear. Although definitions of public interest may vary, *Tunkl* outlined several factors which tend to affect its characterization: (1) the business involved is generally considered suitable for public regulation, or the service is of great importance or necessity to the general public; (2) the party seeking the exculpatory clause has held itself out as willing to serve any or all of the public; (3) the party is often of superior bargaining strength, given the nature of the service; (4) an adhesion type contract is offered with the exculpatory clause; and (5) the person or property is under the control of the party promoting the clause. If a contract meets some or all of this criteria, an exculpatory clause regarding medical malpractice is likely to be held invalid.

C. ARBITRATION PROVISIONS

Arbitration provisions, in contrast to exculpatory clauses, address the method through which compensation of an injury will be determined rather than attempt to avoid liability. Agreements to arbitrate may be made between the parties or pursuant to legislation. In either case, these agreements generally constitute a viable alternative to litigation. Consideration may be given to whether or not they constitute contracts of adhesion. In *Morris v. Metriyakool* (Mich.1984), upon admission to the hospital, a patient was offered an agreement that any dispute arising out of her medical care would be submitted to arbitration. Michigan's Medical Malpractice Arbitration Act permitted such a provision. The court held that the Act did not violate due process and therefore was not unconstitutional.

Michigan's Medical Malpractice Arbitration Act is representative of a number of recent statutory schemes that are designed to deal with the litigation crisis that has resulted from large numbers of malpractice actions. The Michigan act requires that submission to arbitration must be voluntary in that an agreement which contains such a provision must (a) highlight the arbitration clause, (b) make it optional and (c) make it revocable within some limited period of time. If arbitration is accepted, the composition of the tribunal must be fair, and basic requirements of due process must be met. See *Morris*.

V. IMMUNITIES

Through tradition and common law, medical institutions and certain of their personnel have been afforded either absolute or qualified immunity based upon the nature and position of the institution, the source of its funding and available sources of malpractice insurance. The policy reasons promoting immunity typically reflected the need to protect hospitals or medical personnel who provided necessary and even gratuitous medical care from the burdens of tort claims and expensive insurance policies, the cost of which might divert the institution's funds from provision of medical care. Typically, immunity was afforded to charitable institutions as well governmental entities, both at the state and federal level.

A.   CHARITABLE IMMUNITY

Historically, the doctrine of charitable immunity applied to non-profit charitable institutions, the typical classification of most hospitals. This immunity from tort claims was provided in recognition of their limited sources of funding, and in consideration of their efforts to provide medical care for all regardless of ability to pay. As hospitals evolved from charitable institutions to multi-million dollar corporate entities, the need for charitable immunity slowly eroded. The need to encourage medical care to be provided according to standards of due care, along with a recognition that injured parties should not be required to remain uncompensated, caused the doctrine of charitable immunity to be abrogated in varying degrees within most jurisdictions.

Total abrogation of charitable immunity has occurred in a majority of states, while some have limited liability to a certain dollar amount, or in accordance with the hospital's liability insurance. Massachusetts, for example, limits the liability of its hospitals to $20,000 per occurrence, thus retaining charitable immunity beyond that extent. The total or partial abrogation of the doctrine reflects a legislative effort to balance the competing interests of the injured party and the medical institution. For example, in *Peters v. McCalla* (D.S.C.1978), the court stated that

> "[o]ne would have to ignore the realities of business and commerce to suggest that these reasonable rates (of insurance) will not skyrocket with the fall of the doctrine of charitable immunity. There is no better example of what the hospitals in this state can expect to occur in regard to their insurance rates than the tremendous rise in cost of medical malpractice for doctors over the past several years in response to the increased number of malpractice claims brought in the courts of this state."

Consequently, South Carolina abrogated charitable immunity in such cases that an injured patient could show a reckless disregard of the patient's rights. Similarly, other states have abrogated immunity only in cases of wanton or willful misconduct, or gross negligence. See *Seiderman v. American Institute for Mental Studies* (D.N.J.1987).

Seiderman also demonstrated that a jurisdiction can apply charitable immunity doctrine to an institution in another state. *Seiderman* held that New Jersey's charitable immunity doctrine applied to an out-of-state charitable, non-profit institution, *which had contact* with New Jersey by conducting non-profit activities within the state. The doctrine was held to bar a claim by a New Jersey resident against an out-of-state hospital.

B. GOVERNMENTAL IMMUNITY

Like charitable immunity, governmental immunity limits the liability of certain institutions (including hospitals) which are associated with the state or federal government. Like charitable immunity, governmental immunity has also seen substantial erosion in modern times. This is significant in light of the number of governmental facilities providing medical care. In 1946 the federal government enacted the Federal Torts Claim Act through which it abrogates its own immunity (to the extent of $100,000) and thus consents to be sued for most torts, including medical malpractice.

Government immunity at the state level varies among jurisdictions. An example of state level governmental immunity is highlighted in *Tobias v. Phelps* (Mich.App.1985). Michigan's governmental immunity provision encompasses defendants who, in good faith, act in the course or their employment or authority, or reasonably believe they so act and who perform "discretionary tasks". Difficulty arises, however, in determining which functions are considered "discretionary" and which are considered "ministerial" tasks. Governmental immunity is only granted when the tortfeasor performs a discretionary function. The rule of thumb seems to be that decisions about what medical care is needed is considered "discretionary", but that the act of actually carrying out such decisions is considered "ministerial". Accordingly, *Tobias* held that a state hospital may be liable for the death of a patient in a mental health facility who died from an asthma attack while confined to a "quiet room", if confining the patient to the room was considered a ministerial function. Thus the hospital is not protected by governmental immunity if the jury finds that it was not a discretionary decision which caused the death of the patient.

C. STATUTORY IMMUNITY

In some circumstances more that one set of legislation might affect the liability of certain governmental employees. For example, members of the military and even many federal employees are often precluded from bringing tort actions against the government for service-related injuries. See 1 L. Jayson, Handling Federal Tort Claims, secs. 153–155 (1985). In lieu of tort claims, most military and federal employees are entitled to various administrative benefits for personal injuries.

The context in which statutory immunity arises most frequently is suits against military employees such as doctors or psychiatrists affiliated with a Veteran's Hospital. The policy reasons justifying immunization of military personnel include the consideration that such doctors must also respond to military orders in providing medical care. See *Baker v. Barber* (6th Cir.1982). In *Baker*, three statutory provisions were triggered when a civilian employee attempted to bring suit against army physicians for negligent treatment of a work related injury. The Federal Employee Compensation Act

(FECA) precludes relief under the Federal Torts Claim Act (FTCA) for tort claims, including medical malpractice. The Military Medical Malpractice Statute grants immunity to military physicians, requiring the plaintiff to rely on the FTCA. Recognizing that the various statutory immunities barred all suits, the court pointed out that the employee nevertheless would be compensated under FECA.

CHAPTER SEVEN

VICARIOUS LIABILITY AND MULTIPLE DEFENDANTS

I. IN GENERAL: VICARIOUS TORT LIABILITY

Vicarious liability generally arises from the master-servant or principal-agent relationship created through employment or contract. The doctrine holds that a principal may be held liable for the tortious acts of its employees or agents if they acted within the scope of their employment or agency relationship. See generally *Ward v. Gordon* (9th Cir.1993). Other circumstances such as the formation of a partnership or a professional corporation may also subject the principals to vicarious liability.

In the medical field where many licensed independent practitioners function as independent contractors, the question of whether an agency relationship exists becomes a critical determination for purposes of vicarious liability. The finding of an agency relationship generally requires the presence of three distinct elements: (1) some manifestation of consent by the principal that the agent will act on his behalf; (2) acceptance of that undertaking by the agent; and (3) an understanding between the parties that the activities undertaken by the agent are subject to the control of the principal. See generally *Karas v. Jackson* (E.D.Pa.1983).

Manifestation of consent by the principal can be express, as by word or written contract, or implied by the conduct or inaction of the principal. Once the agency relationship is established, the next inquiry is whether the alleged the negligent act of the agent was within the scope of the agency relationship. Such a finding generally requires the following: (1) that the conduct be of the kind that the agent or employee was expected to perform; (2) that the act have occurred substantially within the authorized space and time limits; and (3) that there be involved to some degree an intent to serve the master. See Alfred F. Conrad et al., Enterprise Organizations, sec. 2 (4th ed. 1987). Whether the allegedly negligent activity is within the scope of employment is often determined in part by the codes of professional conduct and provider policies.

Vicarious liability is generally found in employment situations, and is the basis for such doctrines as the so-called "borrowed servants" and "captain of the ship" as well as respondeat superior, infra. In all of these relationships, the actor is primarily responsible for his own negligence. If a principal is vicariously liable, one of two situations is likely to result: either the employee or agent will seek indemnification from the principal, or the original action will name multiple defendants who will sort out liability if and when a judgment is rendered against them.

A. THE "BORROWED SERVANT" RULE

One basis for the "borrowed servant" rule, a special rule of agency which holds principals liable for the negligence of their agents under the doctrine of respondeat superior, is the Restatement (Agency) 2d sec. 227. According to the Restatement, a servant in the general employ of one master or principal (e.g. the hospital) can be also in the special employ of another (e.g. a specific staff physician) for a particular purpose. In those cases in which the doctrine applies, the master, whose business purpose is forwarded by the loaned servant, will be responsible for any tortious acts committed within the scope of the agency. Under certain circumstances, the physician who borrows the servant may also be responsible for his negligence.

The borrowed servant doctrine, however, is not without limits, even in those jurisdictions which recognize it. In *Bernardi v. Community Hospital Association* (Colo.1968), a physician ordered an injection to be given by a nurse which ultimately caused the patient to suffer permanent loss of the normal function of her right foot. The physician was not present during the administration of the injection. As the injection was a nursing function to be performed within the general scope of her employment, only she and her employer would be responsible. The nurse in *Bernardi* was not be held to be a loaned servant of the physician because the physician did not have control over the administration of the injection.

Whether there exists a "right of control" generally determines whether the servant has been "borrowed" by a temporary, second master. In *Sparger v. Worley Hospital* (Tex.1977), a borrowed employee was defined as "one, who, while in the general employment of the hospital, is subject to the right of the physician to direct or control the details of the particular work inquired about, and is not merely cooperating with suggestions of said physician." In *Sparger*, an action was brought against a surgeon for injury resulting when a sponge was left in a patient's body during surgery. The nurses responsible for the sponge count were found by the jury not to be the "borrowed servants" of the surgeon. The court determined it was a jury question upon which reasonable minds could differ as to whether the surgeon "directed" the sponge count. Specific duties concerning this procedure were outlined for the nurses in the hospital procedure manual. The case was ultimately remanded to determine if the finding that the nurses were not borrowed servants was against the great weight of the evidence.

In *Rogers v. Duke* (Tex.App.1989), the court affirmed summary judgment for the physician upon similar facts, holding that the operating room nurses were not the borrowed servants of the surgeon. In *Rogers*, however, the surgeon had already left the operating room when the sponge count was done. The reviewing court relied on factors presented in *Sparger* which supported the finding that the nurses were not borrowed servants: "(1) the defendant-physician did not participate in selection of the nurses; (2) the hospital's policy and procedure manual detailed the duties of the circulating and scrub nurses, including general instructions that applied to both nurses; (3) the sponge count procedures were intended to be used without regard to which surgeon was performing an operation; (4) the defendant-physician did not direct the nurses to make a sponge count." On the basis of the above factors, and the fact that the surgeon was *not present* to supervise at the close of surgery, the court affirmed summary judgment. No jury determination was necessary to resolve the issue of whether the nurses were borrowed servants of the physician.

Two issues emerge in the analysis of the borrowed servant rule: (1) whether the physician had the right to control or actually assumed control; and (2) assuming he did, whether both masters can be held responsible. Courts differ in their approach to these issues.

Sparger required that the physician have only a right of control, while some other courts require that the physician have actually assumed control. Among the latter, presence of the physician when the negligence occurs is particularly significant. *Kitto v. Gilbert* (Colo.App.1977), held that a physician is liable for the acts of hospital employees assisting during the surgery where he had assumed control at the time the negligent act allegedly occurs. In *Kitto*, a patient, while inadequately anesthetized, coughed. The cough resulted in the tube delivering the anesthesia to become disconnected during the preparation for surgery, eventually in the loss of one of the patient's eyes. The court held that the surgeon could be held responsible for negligence of the hospital employees if he had assumed control of the operating room. Thus, if such control was found, the physician, rather than the hospital, would be held liable.

A Washington court also addressed the question of whether a borrowed servant was no longer within the control of his original master. See *Ward v. Gordon* (9th Cir.1993). *Ward* involved the alleged negligence of a military physician who was serving a six month residency at a private hospital. Federal law would preclude personal liability for the physician if it were found that he was acting within the scope of the government's employment. The ninth circuit affirmed the district court's finding that the physician was a borrowed servant of the private hospital. The status of borrowed servant was determined by four factors:

"(1) whether the borrowing master has the right to hire and fire the servant; (2) whether the borrowing master has the right to direct the manner in which the servant performs his duties; (3) whether the value of any equipment the servant brings with him has any bearing on the servant's continued relationship with the borrowing master; and (4) whether the borrowing master exclusively controls or has the exclusive right to control the servant."

Once again, the court held that the right to control (as opposed to actual control) was the pertinent issue.

Ward is consistent with the position of the Restatement (Agency) 2d sec. 226, which provides that it is possible for a person to be a servant of two masters if service to the new master does not involve abandonment of service to the original. In *Ward*, the physician was able to concurrently perform his duties for both the private hospital and the government. Therefore, federal law provided him with immunity from personal liability, although the United States, as the original master, could be held liable for his negligence while practicing at the private hospital.

In suits not involving protected federal employees, both masters are potentially responsible for the negligence of the servant. As explained in the Florida case of *Abraham v. United States* (11th Cir.1991), there is a presumption that a borrowed servant remains in the general employ of his original master, as long as he still performs the master's business. In cases involving medical personnel, it is not uncommon for a single act to benefit two masters, or for liability to be incurred on behalf of both.

B. PHYSICIAN LIABILITY UNDER RESPONDEAT SUPERIOR

Physicians who practice in hospitals are generally not employees but independent contractors. Traditionally they exercise absolute control over the course of the medical care that they provide to their patients.　This right of control, particularly for surgeons using the operating room, has resulted in various rules of liability.　One is an adaptation of the borrowed servant rule, supra, known as the "captain of the ship" doctrine.　Under this doctrine, it is assumed that the surgeon (like the naval captain) has complete control over the operation and the medical personnel (or "crew") who assist in the surgery.　Pursuant to this doctrine, the surgeon or physician, merely by virtue of his presence in the operating room, is responsible for the actions, including the negligence of all persons working "under his command".　See *Sparger v. Worley Hospital* (Tex.1977).　*Sparger* rejected the "captain of the ship" doctrine, finding it to be a false special rule of agency and instead relied upon traditional agency principles, particularly the borrowed servant doctrine.

Physician liability under respondeat superior is more clearly applicable if an employee of the physician such as a nurse or technician acts negligently. Nevertheless, the physician is also potentially responsible for non-employee personnel under agency principles such as the "borrowed servant" rule. Moreover, the fact that the physician is not present when the negligent act occurs does not necessarily exonerate him from responsibility.

Karas v. Jackson (E.D.Pa.1983), provides some guidelines for determining the conditions under which liability may be imposed.　Karas involved the death of a woman during what was alleged to be negligence in the performance of amniocentesis. The plaintiff-husband attempted to hold the director of the Division of Medical Genetics responsible for failing to warn his wife of the risks of the procedure, failing to exercise due care, and failing to perform the procedure in a proper and safe manner. Liability was alleged even though the director was not directly involved in patient care. *Karas*. Vicarious liability was alleged on the basis of respondeat superior, which requires the presence of an agency relationship. In order to find such a relationship, the court held that there must be both a manifestation of consent to act on the physician's behalf, and acceptance of the task by the agent. The court also held, however, that the act must be *subject to the control of the physician*. *Karas* refused to hold the physician-director liable for the death of the patient. Although he may have been involved in "establishing general guidelines for the recommendation or performance of the amniocentesis procedure" the court found that he was not "in charge". He did not employ the physician who performed the procedure, received no benefit from it, and did not direct the actual procedure which resulted in the patient's death.

Hunnicutt v. Wright (5th Cir.1993) also supports the notion that an agency relationship is required, including a certain degree of control. The fifth circuit reversed a district court decision holding a surgeon liable for the negligence of the scrub nurse in failing to inspect an instrument. As a result of the negligence, a screw and washer were left in the chest of the patient. The court held that although the doctor may also have been negligent, he was not liable for the acts or omissions of the nurse if she was not subject to his direction and control. Where the nature of the task (inspecting instruments) requires it to be performed out of the presence of the surgeon and does not require his "specialized medical knowledge", negligence may be imputed to the hospital, but not the surgeon. The hospital was vicariously liable for the negligence of its employee (the nurse) for acts within the scope of her employment, including the inspection of instruments. She was not, however, a borrowed servant for that purpose.

Although the presence of the physician is generally required in order for a court to find that he exercised the requisite degree of control, there are exceptions to the rule. For example, in *Walstad v. Univ. of Minnesota Hospitals* (8th Cir.1971) the appeals court found the physician vicariously liable under principles of respondeat superior for the negligent act of a nurse in administering penicillin to a patient. The patient had a known allergy to the drug. The court imputed liability for this negligence to the physician even though he was not present when the medication was given. Liability resulted because nurses can only administer drugs upon an order of the physician, and he should have known of the allergy. Thus, the physician was held to have exerted the requisite control through the written orders left for the hospital personnel.

Notwithstanding *Walstad*, it is certainly not inevitable that physicians will be held for the manner in which their orders are carried out. In *Bernardi*, supra, a physician was not held liable for ordering an injection to be given by a nurse which ultimately caused the patient to suffer permanent loss of the normal function of her right foot. The injection was apparently given near the sciatic nerve, causing injury to this nerve. See *Bernardi v. Community Hospital Association* (Colo.1968). The physician was again not present during the administration of the injection, but this time was not held liable, even though he had given the order. Respondeat superior was not applicable since the act involved the negligent *administration* of an injection which the physician had no opportunity to control. The nurse was employed by the hospital, and the physician had no opportunity to choose which staff member would administer the drug. He was also not present in order to control the technique. In this situation, the physician's order was not negligent, and his instructions alone did not create a master-servant relationship.

C. PHYSICIAN LIABILITY FOR OTHER PHYSICIANS

The basic principle regarding physician liability for acts of another physician is that no liability will result unless there is control over such other physician. See *Karas*. The requirement of control, which might be present in an employment or agency relationship, is necessary for vicarious liability. For example, in *Royer v. St. Paul Fire and Marine Ins. Co.* (La.App.1987), the court held that a surgeon "was not vicariously liable for alleged negligence on the part of radiologist in performing an arteriogram on plaintiff's decedent under principles of respondeat superior, as neither physician was agent, servant, or employee of the other and two physicians practiced different types of medicine completely independent of each other."

When consultation with a specialist is involved in the care of a patient, the question arises as to whether the primary physician might be liable for the negligence of a consultant. Often it depends upon the particular fact situation, as well as the law of the jurisdiction. It may also depend upon the extent of simultaneous involvement with the patient and whether the care rendered by either physician was entirely independent of the other.

In *Largess v. Tatem* (Vt.1972), the original physician, a general practitioner, admitted a woman to the hospital for a fracture of her left hip. After initially treating the patient, he referred her to a specialist in orthopedic surgery who successfully repaired the patient's hip. After the surgery the specialist arranged for the patient to receive physical therapy, and instructed that there be no weight bearing on the operative hip. The surgeon then allowed the patient's care to be resumed by the general practitioner. When she was discharged by the general practitioner, however, he neglected to advise against full weight bearing on the operative hip. The result was a failure of the fixation device and a second operation to repair the damage.

In *Largess*, the general practitioner was found liable even though the surgeon had not left specific discharge instructions for the patient. Although the surgeon had permitted the general practitioner to take over the patient's post-operative care, the general practitioner should have known, on the basis of the surgeon's notes and his own expertise, that weight bearing could cause danger to the patient. Furthermore, if he was uncertain about discharge instructions, he should have consulted with the specialist. As stated by the court, "voluntary ignorance affords no protection from legal liability."

In contrast to *Largess*, the third circuit held there was no liability for the alleged negligence of a consultant. In *Suire v. Lake Charles Memorial Hospital* (La.App.1991), a neurosurgeon requested a consultation with an internist when post-operatively, his patient showed signs of a rare infection. The court found that the neurosurgeon deferred to the judgment of the internist, and therefore was not liable for any negligence that might have occurred.

Courts have held that a referring physician generally is not liable for negligence in the consulting physician's care "unless there is some control in the course of the treatment of one by the other, agency or concert of action, or negligence in the referral." Concert of action means that both physicians continue to treat the patient (and charge for patient visits), or that the referring physician remains present during the patient's treatment, thus retaining some control over the course of treatment provided to the patient.

Where one physician "covers" for another, i.e. treats another physician's patients on a rotating basis during vacations, week-ends or other "on-call" time, there is generally no liability imposed on the regular physician for the negligence of the covering physician. In *Kavanaugh by Gonzales v. Nussbaum* (N.Y.1988), for example, the court held that an obstetrician was not vicariously liable for injury to a baby born in distress as a result of complications from an undiagnosed condition of the placenta. Although the court found that the "covering" or "on-call" arrangement was mutually beneficial, there was no agency relationship because there did not exist any element of control. The court examined the policy concerns that weighed against extending vicarious liability to the covering physician. Rotating coverage is necessary for the continual patient care around the clock. Imposing liability on a physician merely because he participates in an on-call arrangement would discourage practice in certain specialties, and tends to increase the cost of medical care, both of which are detrimental to the public interest.

Steinberg v. Dunseth (Ill.App.1994), followed the reasoning of *Kavanaugh* in declining to hold physicians liable for negligence resulting from coverage arrangements. In both, a woman died from complications resulting from an allegedly negligent surgical procedure performed by a covering surgeon.

The court refused, however, to hold the regular surgeon liable unless there was evidence of his own negligence in selecting an incompetent covering physician.

Negligent selection of a physician to work in collaboration to perform surgery may also lead to liability. For example, *Kitto v. Gilbert* (Colo.App. 1977) held the surgeon liable for the actions of the anesthesiologist whom he had selected for the procedure. But while negligence in the selection of another physician may lead to liability, it requires that the selecting physician have knowledge of the other's negligent propensities and thereafter fail to address the problem. Alternatively, if he fails to make reasonable inquiry about the competence of a physician he selects, he may also become liable for any injury caused by such other physician. The physician-patient relationship thus creates a duty not only to perform non-negligently but also to select others who would be expected to perform competently.

A number of jurisdictions would also hold a physician liable for successive acts of malpractice based on the position of the Restatement (Second) of Torts § 457 (1965). This means that a physician who performs negligently may also be liable for any injury resulting from the malpractice of a subsequent physician whose treatment was sought to repair the injury caused by the initial negligence. Liability will not be imposed on such initial physician for care which is considered to be independent of his treatment. In order to be held liable, the care of the initial physician must result in an identifiable harm which the subsequent physician's efforts were intended to address. See *Daly v. United States*.

II. PARTNERSHIPS AND PROFESSIONAL CORPORATIONS

A. THE PARTNERSHIP

At common law the partnership was the predominant form of professional association utilized by medical practitioners. A partnership can arise without any express verbal or written agreement by the partners. A majority of jurisdictions have adopted the Uniform Partnership Act of 1914 (in its revised form) which is considered to be a "default" statute to provide guidance for issues that arise within the partnership, even in the absence of any agreement. See Enterprise Organizations, supra.

Where there exists a partnership arrangement, express or implied, liability of the partners is joint and several. When an individual partner is sued, he need not be the actual tortfeasor; he may be a partner of the tortfeasor who had no personal involvement at all. See *Zuckerman v. Antenucci* (N.Y.Sup.1984). As explained by one court, "on the principle of mutual agency, the partnership, or every member of a partnership, is liable for torts committed by one of the members acting in the scope of the firm business although they do not participate in, ratify or have knowledge of such torts." *Schmitz v. St. Lukes Hospital, Inc. et al.*

(D.N.D.1966). Therefore, the implication is that within this arrangement the plaintiff may bring an action against the partnership or any individual partner; it is not necessary to join all the members to ensure compensation in the event that a judgment is rendered.

At least one court has attempted to refine the concept of joint and several liability to better reflect the intent of partnership liability. The court held that a physician not involved in the particular negligent act could be dismissed individually from a lawsuit involving a partner or the partnership. Such a physician would not liable in his individual capacity for the tort of his partner, although he would be liable in his capacity as a partner of the professional association. See *Keech v. Mead Johnson and Co.* (Pa.Super.1990).

Partners may also be held liable for the negligence of their employees or agents. For example, in *Brown v. Moore* (3d Cir.1957), the federal district court held that partners who maintained a sanitarium could be liable for the negligence of its medical director which resulted in the death of a patient, if the director was an agent of the owners of the sanitarium. Respondeat superior would apply and the negligence of the employee or agent would be imputed to the partners.

B. THE PROFESSIONAL CORPORATION

The corporation (including the professional corporation) is an alternate form of professional association which can be selected for organizational purposes. The liability of the members of the corporation (the shareholders), and the corporation itself is governed by the corporate laws of the state of incorporation. All states have specific statutes which govern incorporation and include the common forms of organization for health providers. The decision of an individual physician about whether to incorporate is generally based upon the cost of doing so, as well as the particular features of the applicable law. Generally, the larger the group of practitioners, the more advantageous it will be to form a corporation.

The major incentive for incorporation is that it limits the liability of its members to the value of the assets of the corporation. The corporation will not shield a physician from liability for his own negligence, but usually will protect an individual doctor from liability for the medical malpractice of another physician in the corporation. See Health Care in the '90s and Beyond: Practice Structure, Competition, Government Regulation, and Malpractice Concerns, C470 ALI–ABA 41 (1989). On the other hand, the corporation may be held liable for the negligence of an individual member under respondeat superior or an agency theory. See *McGuire v. Sifers* (Kan.1984), *Medi–Stat, Inc. v. Kusturin* (Ark. 1990). Depending upon the jurisdiction, the corporation itself may or may not need to be insured for the negligence of an individual member.

A related liability issue is whether a corporate stockholder, director, agent or employee of the corporation would be personally liable for torts of a physician member of the corporation. For example, patients have attempted to sue individually non-treating physicians who were members of a professional corporation for the malpractice of a physician with whom they were associated. *Birt v. St. Mary Mercy Hospital of Gary, Inc. et al.* (Ind.App.1977) involved a medical corporation of physicians which was hired to staff the emergency room of the hospital. The plaintiff alleged that he was treated negligently by one of the corporation's physicians. The court held that physicians associated with the treating physician were not individually liable for negligence merely by virtue of being officers or having holdings in the corporation. Individual liability would require malfeasance on the part of the individual physician. *Birt's* interpretation of the statute was consistent with the common law of the Indiana.

In some situations, the negligence of a physician results in suit against an organization with which he is not directly associated nor maintains employee status. For example, a managing corporation operating on behalf of a hospital may or may not be liable for the negligence of a physician who treats patients at the hospital. Such liability usually depends upon agency principles, i.e., whether the management corporation has the requisite degree of supervision and control over the physician. See *Noble v. Porter* (N.Y.A.D.1992).

As discussed, the scope of liability of a corporation and its members will depend upon common law and statutory provisions, as well as the particular facts of the case. In addition, principles of agency may be applied in those cases where a negligent physician is not a member of the corporation. In any event, the corporate form of organization does minimize individual liability on behalf of a member who does not in any way participate in another member's negligent act.

III. LIABILITY OF THE HEALTH MAINTENANCE ORGANIZA- TIONS

A Health Maintenance Organization (HMO) is an alternative to the traditional form of health care organizations. It has been defined as:

"an organized system of health care which provides or arranges for a comprehensive array of basic and supplemental health care services. These services are provided on a prepaid basis to voluntarily enrolled members living within a prescribed geographic area. Responsibility for the delivery, quality and payment of health care falls to the managing organization."

Boyd v. Albert Einstein Medical Center (Pa.Super.1988).

Liability of an HMO for the negligence of physicians who practice within its structure is generally based on a theory of ostensible agency. The court will typically determine whether a physician is an agent of the HMO by finding (1) whether the patient looked to the HMO, rather than to the particular physician, for care; and (2) whether the HMO "holds out" the physician as its agent. Evidence of such an agency relationship might be found in the HMO's literature, as well as its master contract. Summary judgment was denied in *Boyd* on the basis that the vicarious liability of the HMO was an issue of material fact.

A number of more recent cases addressed a more difficult issue: whether all such state law claims are preempted by federal legislation, specifically, the Employment Retirement Income Security Act of 1974, (ERISA). An HMO would qualify as an ERISA plan and be subject to its preemption provision if it satisfies five elements:

"(1) A 'plan, fund or program' (2) established or maintained (3) by an employee organization, or by both, (4) for the purpose of providing medical, surgical, hospital care, sickness, accident, disability, death, unemployment or vacation benefits, apprenticeship or other training programs, day care centers, scholarship funds, pre-paid legal services or severance benefits (5) to the participants or their beneficiaries."

See *McClellan v. Health Maintenance Organization of Penn.* (Pa.Super.1992). Organizations that are considered HMOs vary widely in their organizational structure, benefits and services. Whether a particular HMO would qualify as an ERISA plan depends upon individual circumstances, including such factors as: whether the employees participate in the management of the plan; whether the plan is primarily geared for the marketing of products or services rather than providing insurance benefits; and the extent to which the plan is a direct provider of health care. See *McClellan*; *Butler v. Wu* (D.N.J.1994).

ERISA has a broad preemption clause, recognized by the U.S. Supreme Court to protect participants and beneficiaries. See *Butler v. Wu*. Once it has been determined that an HMO falls under the definition of an ERISA plan, the issue arises as to whether the claim is thus preempted. Section 514(a) of ERISA provides that the provisions supersede the laws of the state that "relate to any employee benefit plan." Thus, as stated in *McClellan*, "[t]he preemptive provision of ERISA was meant to establish pension plan legislation as an exclusively federal concern, reserving for the federal government the sole power to regulate the field of employee benefit plans."

The key test as to whether a claim is preempted by ERISA is whether it "relates to" ERISA. Courts have evaluated that concept on the basis of the nature of the claim, i.e. whether the action was a tort claim alleging the negligence of a physician, or whether it was a contract action challenging such issues as the distribution and administration of benefits. For example, in *McClellan*, one of the claims was alleged negligence in the removal of a patient's mole without performing a biopsy. The patient later died as a result of an undiagnosed malignancy. The court found that the tort claim was not preempted, but that any claim based in contract likely would be so preempted. Similarly, in *Elsesser v. Hospital of the Philadelphia College of Osteopathic Medicine* (E.D.Pa.1992), the court held that claims of vicarious liability arising out of the physician's negligence were not preempted by ERISA; however, a claim for the HMO's refusal to pay for equipment was so preempted. This latter claim relates to the benefits of the plan.

Recent cases have held that negligence-based claims predicated on the vicarious liability of the HMO are likely to be preempted by ERISA. For example, in *Ricci v. Gooberman* (D.N.J.1993), a federal district court in New Jersey held that a claim alleging failure to advise a patient of abnormalities on a mammogram was preempted by ERISA. The court held that this type of claim "related to" the benefit plan because the determination of vicarious liability requires evaluation of the relationship between the physician and the administrative plan under which the latter provided care. In determining the existence of agency relationship upon which to hold the HMO liable, the court would necessarily have to look at the terms of the plan, specifically to the degree of control and payment mechanisms. *Ricci.*

The federal district court in *Dukes v. United States Health Care Systems of Pennsylvania, Inc.* (E.D.Pa.1994) also concluded that the preemption provision of ERISA encompassed both direct claims against HMOs as well as those based upon a theory of ostensible agency. The court held that a claim for medical malpractice involves a breach of promised plan performance, and therefore "relates to" the plan. Again, in evaluating the claim, representations made by the HMO were a significant factor. The court also noted some policy reasons for not holding an HMO liable, such as higher costs resulting from insuring against such claims. *Dukes*.

Finally, in *Butler v. Wu* (D.N.J.1994), the district court articulated similar reasoning to hold that "ERISA preempts state-law tort claims brought against an HMO for the negligence of one of its participating physicians, where the HMO does not itself provide health care services." The court qualified its holding, however, in that it required that the HMO not be a direct provider of care, targeting instead those HMOs which are more like traditional insurers.

CHAPTER EIGHT

HOSPITAL LIABILITY

I. IN GENERAL—THE ROOTS OF HOSPITAL LIABILITY

A. RESPONDEAT SUPERIOR

Historically hospitals, as charitable institutions, were afforded absolute immunity from tort liability. In *Bing v. Thunig* (N.Y.1957), the court provided a succinct summary of what was then the state of the law—as well as its rationale for abandoning the traditional rule. Aside from charitable considerations, the court also rejected hospital liability based on traditional principles of respondeat superior since the staff (physicians, nurses and other skilled professionals) was considered akin to independent contractors. As such, they perform patient care functions with that level of skill required for their profession. Consequently, the hospital, being unable to control these professionals or dictate the course of the treatment provide, could not be held liable for its employees' negligence.

Next, in historical perspective, followed the New York case of *Schloendorff v. Society of N.Y. Hospital* (N.Y.1914). In *Schloendorff* the court held that hospital liability for the negligence of its employees depends on whether the causative act of the injury was "administrative" or "medical". Administrative acts were considered to be those in the realm of hospital control, whereas medical acts were not. This naturally gave rise to many inconsistencies in interpretation of what exactly constituted medical or administrative tasks. Notwithstanding the difficulties in interpretation, the basic underlying issue was whether or not the hospital could be deemed to have any control over the particular act involved.

As the nature and public perception of the hospital institution has changed, liability of the hospital for the negligent acts of its staff has emerged as a viable claim. As the court in *Schloendorff* explained, "hospitals have evolved into highly sophisticated corporations operating primarily on a fee-for-service basis. The corporate hospital of today has assumed the role of a comprehensive health center with responsibility for arranging and coordinating the total health care of its patients." Today, the public expectation of the hospital reaches far beyond providing a facility for medical treatment; it is a full service institution with responsibility for all aspects of patient care.

As clearly established by the New York Court in *Bing v. Thunig* (N.Y.1957), hospitals are no longer exempt from rules of liability based on respondeat superior. In *Bing*, a woman was burned during an operation as a result of a surgeon's use of electrocautery. The bed linen ignited during the operation as it had been contaminated by a zephiren solution during the nurses' preparation of the patient for surgery. The patient sued both the surgeon and the hospital. The court allowed recovery against both, holding that the hospital should bear the same burden as other employers, including responsibility for negligent acts of its employees committed within the scope of their employment. *Bing v. Thunig* (N.Y.1957).

B. EMPLOYEES AND INDEPENDENT CONTRACTORS

Early decisions concerning hospital liability did not address its potential liability for negligence of the professional staff who generally receive no economic compensation from the hospital. These professionals may include the staff physicians who are not paid by the hospital but instead exchange their services for "staff privileges", i.e., the ability to admit patients to the hospital and provide care for them within the hospital. Staff physicians may also include physicians or other professionals who perform certain specialties such as emergency medicine, anesthesia, radiology, or pathology through a contract with the hospital to provide such services. Typically patients are billed directly.

Another variation on the theme occurs when specialty services are performed for the hospital and are compensated on a contract rather than salary basis. For purposes of liability, services performed within these types of arrangements are generally considered to be those of an independent contractor. The critical factor in determining whether such professionals are "employees" or "independent contractors" is the institution's "right to control" their conduct and activity. Restatement (Agency) 2d sec. 2. Since the hospital does not generally retain a right to control the manner in which they practice their profession, (but only to terminate the contract) usually they are deemed to be independent contractors.

In determining whether there is a "right of control" in order to classify a provider of care as an employee or independent contractor, some jurisdictions will consider other factors besides the economic relationship. For example, some will inquire about whether an agency relationship was intended, whether there is independent ownership, whether the service involves a distinct occupation, and whether special skill is needed to perform the work. See *Menzie v. Windham Community Memorial Hospital* (D.Conn.1991). The Restatement (Agency) 2d also considers such factors as whether the worker supplies the tools and instrumentalities needed, the length of time of the employment, and whether the particular occupation is typically done by a specialist without supervision. (Restatement (Agency) 2d sec. 220.)

A few jurisdictions have been reluctant to impute the liability of a physician to the hospital under any circumstance on the basis that hospitals are "powerless" to command or forbid any acts within the professional practice of the physician. See *Banks v. St. Mary's Hospital and Medical Center* (D.Colo. 1983). This, of course, does not preclude the possibility of a negligence action against the hospital based upon its own tortious acts.

II. VICARIOUS LIABILITY

A. OSTENSIBLE OR APPARENT AGENCY

The doctrine of ostensible agency or apparent authority has been the predominant theory upon which to base an action for vicarious liability against a hospital for the negligence of independent contractors. It suggests an exception to the general rule that the hospital incurs no liability for the negligence of independent contractors but only for those who provide care within the traditional employment relationship. In *Jackson v. Power* (Alaska 1987), the court determined that two factors are important in establishing ostensible agency: "(1) whether the patient looks to the institution, rather that the individual physician, for care; and, (2) whether the hospital 'holds out' the physician as its employee." This theory mirrors the Restatement (Second) of Torts (1965) which provides: "One who employs an independent contractor to perform services for another which are accepted in the reasonable belief that the services are being rendered by the employer or by his servants, is subject to liability for physical harm caused by the negligence of the contractor in supplying them himself or by his servants."

Yet another potential basis of liability can be derived from the Restatement (Agency) 2d which recognizes "agency by estoppel". To meet this standard, there must be evidence of justifiable reliance by the patient on the representations of the hospital that care is provided by servants or agents of the hospital. This additional element of reliance makes agency by estoppel a stricter standard than that required by the tort theory of ostensible agency. See *Walker v. Winchester Memorial Hospital* (W.D.Va.1984).

B. NON–DELEGABLE DUTIES

The cases which consistently support the use of the doctrine of ostensible agency are those involving care provided by physicians through the hospital emergency room. One such case involved the alleged wrongful death of a woman treated in a hospital emergency room which was staffed by a group of physicians who delivered emergency services through a contract with the hospital. See *Stewart v. Midani* (N.D.Ga.1981). Several factors were identified to justify a patient assuming that there existed an agency relationship between the hospital and the emergency room group. Specifically, the patient signed a hospital release form; the patient was referred to as a patient of the hospital on the indemnification agreement; the patient was billed by the hospital, with payment to be submitted to the hospital; the appearance of the emergency room was that it was an integral part of the hospital. *Stewart*. These actions were held to indicate that the hospital was representing the physician as its agent.

Other factors will also affect the existence of an agency relationship. A person entering through the emergency room is unaware of the relationships between the health care professionals who care for them, particularly when entering with an emergent or crisis situation. Usually patients cannot be expected to inquire about the facility's organizational structure or to make decisions based upon such inquiry. The *Stewart* court concluded that unless the hospital notifies patients as to the status of its caregivers, or unless patients are treated by their own personal physicians who meet them at the facility, the patient may justifiably rely on the apparent authority of the physicians as agents of the hospital. Therefore, the hospital could be held responsible for any injury resulting from that care. *Stewart.*

In *Walker v. Winchester Memorial Hospital* (W.D.Va.1984), the federal district court found the reasoning of *Stewart* persuasive, finding not only that the hospital "held out" or represented that the physicians were agents of the hospital, but also that the patient relied on that representation to its detriment. The fact that the patient was comatose upon arriving at the emergency room and continued in that condition for several days weighed against a finding of reliance; however, the court left the issue for the jury. The requirement of reliance under agency principles is seemingly more difficult to prove.

A divergence from this stricter standard is illustrated by *Martell v. St. Charles Hospital* (N.Y.Sup.

1987), where the hospital was held to be vicariously liable for the treatment given by physicians in the emergency room. As the court explained, "patients in this situation have looked to the hospital as the provider of medical services, the hospital has given the appearance that it is the provider of the medical services and the patient has reasonably relied on that appearance." The court held, for policy reasons, that agency principles should not be strictly adhered to as they would provide hospitals with a shield against liability. *Martell* held that "the law of New York should be that hospitals are liable for the malpractice of physicians in hospital emergency rooms irrespective of private contractual relationships between the physicians and the hospitals and without regard for whether the patient has reason not to rely upon the appearance that the physician is a hospital employee."

In the same year, *Jackson v. Power* (Alaska 1987), affirmed reliance on basic principles of agency law and also found a basis for potential liability of hospitals for emergency room physicians through traditional exceptions to the non-liability of independent contractors. *Jackson* involved a boy who was injured due to a fall from a cliff. He suffered multiple injuries including internal damage. The emergency room doctor ordered no tests to determine the status of his kidneys and the boy ultimately lost both kidneys. The court pointed out that it was the conduct of the principal (hospital) which caused a third person (patient) to trust that the agent (physician) had the authority to act for the principal. Accordingly, liability was found. The court held that the patient need not prove that the hospital specifically represented that the physician was an employee or that the patient relied upon such representation, unless there was evidence that the patient "knew or should have known" that the treating physician was not an employee.

An established exception to the rule of "no liability" for the negligence of an independent contractor is the finding of a non-delegable duty. This issue arose in *Jackson:* whether the hospital had a non-delegable duty to provide emergency room services. Based on state regulations, the Joint Committee for Accreditation of Hospitals' (JCAH) standards and hospital bylaws, *Jackson* held that a general acute care hospital has a non-delegable duty to provide emergency care. State regulations require that a physician be available to provide emergency care on a 24–hour basis. JCAH mandates that an emergency plan be in place, and that the hospital direct and review the quality of care, as well as provide written policies and procedures for emergency services. The hospital bylaws also provided for the regulation and supervision of the emergency department. The result was that the duty was found to be non-delegable, and the hospital was liable for the adverse consequences of any negligent care provided.

The principle that a hospital incurs duties that are non-delegable has been applied to other medical specialties such as anesthesia and radiology. Application of the theory of ostensible agency has been variable. For instance, in *Gamble v. United States*

(N.D.Ohio 1986), a patient died following what was believed to have been a cardiorespiratory arrest incident to endotracheal intubation during surgery at a Veteran's Administration hospital. The anesthesia services were provided independently through a contract with the Veteran's Administration. As the hospital held itself out as a full-service institution, including a provider of anesthesia, the court held that it could be liable for negligent provision of services. The hospital was held to have induced patients to rely on the full care provided by the hospital. Additionally, the anesthesiologist involved was the Chief of Anesthesia who also maintained an office within the hospital.

On the other hand, in *Menzie v. Windham Community Memorial Hospital* (D.Conn.1991), the court found no liability on the part of the hospital for negligent anesthesia services provided by the so-called independent contractors. These independent contractors received no compensation or benefits from the hospital and carried their own malpractice insurance. The court found that the hospital did not exert any control over their practice, since only an executive committee of staff doctors evaluated the quality of their care. The hospital did not do so directly. The court held that the hospital could not be held liable on an apparent agency theory as the requisite element of reliance was absent. Additionally, the court appeared to require direct evidence of reliance such as the hospital leading patients to believe that the physicians were employees. *Menzie* further held that the hospital did not have a non-delegable duty to provide anesthesia or other services. The court found only that "[t]he hospital's duty is to provide a place for treatment and ensure the availability of treatment."

The varying rules applicable to anesthesiology appear to also apply to radiology. Thus liability for radiology services will not typically be imposed on the hospital if provided by independent contractors. For instance, in *Royer v. St. Paul Fire & Marine Insurance Co.* (La.App.1987), the court held there was no vicarious liability of the hospital on behalf of a radiologist who was allegedly negligent while performing an arteriogram. The hospital had a contract with an independent radiology clinic which provided equipment, employed its own technicians and handled its own billing, insurance, and workmen's compensation. Principles of non-delegable duty were also rejected.

In another case involving a radiologist in a rural area who travelled from hospital to hospital, a Montana court refused to find an agency relationship despite the hospital having provided the radiologist with an office, equipment and personnel, and handling all of the billing. The court declined to find liability under a theory of vicarious liability for a non-delegable duty. See *Estates of Milliron v. Francke* (Mont.1990). This, of course, does not necessarily mean that a radiologist employed by a hospital who performs negligently might not subject the hospital to liability under principles of vicarious liability. See *Daly v. United States* (9th Cir.1991).

C. SCOPE OF LIABILITY

Under some circumstances, a hospital may be held vicariously liable for the negligence of a physician outside of the scope of the traditional physician-patient relationship. For example, a duty to warn the patient of an abnormality detected during an employment physical exam was imposed in *Daly v. United States* (9th Cir.1991). In *Daly*, a Veteran's Administration hospital radiologist neglected to inform a patient of the results of an x-ray taken during a routine physical examination. The patient later suffered permanent lung damage which could have been avoided had the condition been diagnosed in a timely manner. The court held that the Veteran's Administration hospital could also be held liable for injury resulting from negligence. To the extent that the physicians may be liable under such circumstances, liability may also extend to a hospital with whom the physician has the requisite relationship.

D. THE *PETRILLO* DOCTRINE

In defending a hospital against a claim of vicarious liability for injury resulting from its physicians' negligent care, there are certain procedural considerations that may become significant. The landmark case of *Petrillo v. Syntex Laboratories* (Ill.App. 1986), involved a fall of a patient from a gurney due to the negligence of a hospital employee. The hospital's attorney discussed the matter with the patient's treating physician. Criticizing that discussion, the *Petrillo* court held that "the defense attorney's *ex parte* discussions with patient's treating physicians which were done without the patient's consent and which were not performed pursuant to authorized methods of discovery, violated public policy favoring physician-patient confidentiality as reflected in the code of ethics of medical profession and favoring fiduciary nature of relationship between patient and treating physician."

Petrillo, however, has subsequently been limited in its application by *Morgan v. Count of Cook* (Ill. App.1993). In *Morgan*, where the hospital and physician were both defendants, the court held that the hospital is included within the physician-patient privilege, as the patient is deemed to have impliedly consented to the release of his medical information to the hospital. Thus in *Morgan, ex parte* discussions between the patient's treating physician and counsel for the hospital were permissible.

The distinction, of course, was that *Morgan* involved a situation where the hospital was defending itself against actions of its own physician who treated the patient, as opposed to *Petrillo* which dealt with the hospital defending itself for the actions of its employee. The *Petrillo* rule places the hospital in a difficult situation: the hospital must go through the formalities of discovery and may not even be able to acquire the information needed to defend itself. The defense attorneys are barred from communicating directly with the physician (whose own actions may have contributed to the injury). To avoid this disadvantage to the defense,

Morgan held that since the hospital is vicariously liable for the conduct of a physician, the physician-patient privilege is impliedly waived. Therefore, attorneys defending the hospital for such acts of negligence would have free access to communicate with the physician.

III. CORPORATE RESPONSIBILITY
A. GENERAL DUTY OF CARE, CUSTODY AND SUPERVISION

Generally, the theory of corporate liability of a hospital is based upon a duty of care, custody and supervision by the hospital and its staff to its patients. Although this duty will typically be carried out by one or more individual staff members, the hospital may be directly responsible to the patient for ensuring the staff is adequately selected, trained and monitored.

As one court pointed out, the hospital does not insure the safety of the patient who is admitted to the hospital, but it does insure that patient care is conducted in accordance with reasonable standards consistent with the condition of the patient. See *Mounds Park Hospital v. Von Eye* (8th Cir.1957). These duties may include the exercise of ordinary care in the custody and supervision of the patient. For example, the court in *Mounds Park* held the hospital negligent when a patient jumped from a second floor window after orders were left by the physicians to observe the patient closely.

In *Wooten v. United States* (W.D.Tenn.1982), the court held the hospital's duty of reasonable care was breached when a patient was permitted to leave his bed and subsequently fell. The hospital's liability resulted from failure to raise the side rails on the patient's bed in view of the age, condition, and medication requirements of the patient. Thus, today the hospital does more than furnish a facility for care and treatment; it is directly involved in the care and management of patients.

This duty may also encompass other health and safety concerns such as providing wholesome food, protecting patients from assault and the spread of communicable disease, and ensuring that patients are in a safe building with adequate ventilation and emergency exits.

B. DUTY TO PROVIDE EQUIPMENT AND SUPPLIES

Often reasonable and adequate care of the patient depends upon the availability of adequate equipment and supplies. In *Emory University v. Porter* (Ga.App.1961), the court clearly articulated the majority rule concerning equipment and supplies. In *Porter*, an infant, lying in a heated incubator, was burned on the foot by a light bulb inside the incubator. The incubator was an older model which allegedly did not provide precise heat control or shielding from the heat mechanism. Although the unit was under the control of the attending physician, the plaintiff did not allege negligence on his behalf.

The court held that the hospital was not required to furnish the latest or most up-to-date equipment, or to incorporate all possible improvements in existing equipment. According to that court, the appliance, which was not state of the art, was not necessarily defective.

C. LIABILITY FOR CORPORATE NEGLIGENCE

The theory of corporate negligence, as originally introduced in 1964, has expanded hospital liability for the medical care and patient services provided by physicians or others, including employees and independent contractors. Pursuant to the theory the hospital is charged with certain responsibilities that are owed directly to the patient regarding services provided within the facility.

The leading case establishing the theory of corporate negligence is *Darling v. Charleston Community Memorial Hospital* (Ill.1965). *Darling* involved a boy with multiple leg fractures who was treated by an on-call emergency room physician. The physician applied a plaster cast and admitted the patient to the hospital, but the physician never consulted an orthopedist to review his treatment. Within days, the nurses observed that the patient's toes became dark in color, swollen and a strong odor was emitted from the cast. Although adjustments were made in the cast by the same physician, the condition of the leg worsened. When the patient was finally transferred to another hospital, the leg had become gangrenous and ultimately had to be amputated eight inches below the knee.

In the suit that followed, the plaintiff brought an action directly against the hospital where he was originally treated. The patient alleged that the professional competency of the medical and nursing staff was the responsibility of the hospital. In particular, the plaintiff alleged that the emergency room physician was not trained to treat a complicated fracture, and he should have consulted a specialist. The plaintiff's position was that the duty of care of a licensed and accredited facility was established by licensing regulations, accreditation standards, and its own bylaws. As noted by the court, these administrative guidelines help define the standard of conduct necessary to fulfill that duty. Neither custom nor regulations were held to be conclusive in establishing a duty, but the rules and regulations may help the jury decide what was feasible and what the hospital knew or should have known concerning its responsibilities for the patient.

In *Darling*, the allegations, which were supported by the regulations, standards and the bylaws of the hospital, were that the hospital failed to have sufficient nurses trained to recognize the gangrenous condition of the leg. Further, the hospital failed to require consultation or review of the treatment rendered by the on-call emergency room physician. According to the court, either of these grounds would support the jury verdict that the hospital was negligent.

Subsequent cases have classified the duties of the hospital into four general areas. These are: (1) a duty to use reasonable care in the maintenance of safe and adequate facilities and equipment; (2) a duty to select and retain only competent physicians; (3) a duty to oversee all persons who practice medicine or engage in patient care; and (4) a duty to formulate, adopt and enforce adequate rules and policies to ensure quality care for all patients. See *Thompson v. Nason Hospital* (Pa.1991).

The duty to select and retain only competent physicians was illustrated in *Purcell v. Zimbelman* (Ariz.App.1972). In *Purcell*, the plaintiff brought a malpractice action against a physician treating his condition, and against the hospital for granting staff privileges to a physician whom it should have known was not competent. According to *Purcell*, the hospital owes certain duties directly to a patient, which are defined as non-delegable by licensing regulations, accreditation standards and hospital bylaws. In an accredited facility, the governing body (i.e., board of trustees) has ultimate responsibility for the quality of patient care. If, as in *Purcell*, the hospital assigns review and/or supervision of the physicians to a particular department, such assignment does not release the hospital from direct responsibility and liability for negligence. The court held that "the department of surgery was acting for and on behalf of the hospital in fulfilling this duty and if the department was negligent in not taking any action against Purcell or recommending to the board of trustees that action would be taken, then the hospital would also be negligent."

In order for the hospital to become liable under a theory of corporate negligence, there must be evidence that it had actual or constructive notice of the defect or process which created the harm. Actual or constructive notice may be obtained through information regarding staff physicians' patient care, peer review procedures, previous complaints, lawsuits or other evidence of substandard care. Additionally, the negligence attributed to the hospital must be found to have been a substantial factor in bringing about the harm to the patient. See *Thompson*.

In *Purcell*, the surgeon performed a particular procedure on a patient without waiting for the results of a biopsy or frozen section. The patient actually had a less serious condition which warranted a less drastic procedure. As a result, the patient suffered the loss of a kidney, a permanent colostomy, and urinary problems. The court admitted testimony regarding two prior malpractice suits against the surgeon. They were held to be evidence of notice to the hospital that the doctor was unskilled in this area. According to the court, it was customary for hospitals to review, through committees, the practice of staff physicians and to restrict or suspend those who do not demonstrate competency in a particular area. Again, this duty is nondelegable and ultimately remains the responsibility of the hospital. See *Purcell*.

The operation of the notice requirement is illustrated in *Thompson v. Nason Hospital* (Pa.1991). In *Thompson*, a woman was transported to the hospital emergency room following a car accident. Due to multiple trauma and a history of heart disease, she was admitted to the intensive care unit. The next day the patient was unable to move her left foot due to an intracerebral hematoma. The surgeon, however, attributed this to a neurological problem and did not investigate further despite the fact the patient was on anticoagulants and exhibiting bleeding in her eye. See *Thompson*.

The court stated that if a physician fails to act after abnormalities are reported, custom and hospital policy should require that the situation be reported to the authorities of the hospital so that corrective action can be taken. *Thompson*. Such a requirement would put the hospital on constructive notice that the physician was not handling the patient appropriately. If, for example, there had been a failure to report a variation from standard practice and the patient was injured as a result, liability of the hospital may result.

To establish liability on the part of a hospital, causation must also be proven. According to *Purcell*, the plaintiff "must introduce evidence that it was more likely than not that the conduct of the defendant was a substantial factor in bringing about the result." Thus, the plaintiff must prove that the negligence of the hospital was "substantial" in causing the injury. As *Purcell*, stated, "[w]e believe it reasonably probable to conclude that had the hospital taken some action against Dr. Purcell, whether in the form of suspension, remonstration, restriction or other means, the surgical procedure utilized in this case would not have been undertaken by the doctor and Mr. Zimbelman would not have been injured."

The requirements of notice and causation potentially limit the liability of the hospital even where negligence on the part of the physician or the hospital is found. For example, in *Bost v. Riley* (N.C.App.1980), where a physician failed to keep adequate progress notes, the court found that the hospital violated its duty in not taking appropriate corrective action. However, as no evidence was offered that this omission contributed to the death of the patient, the hospital could not be held liable. See also *Walls v. Hazleton State General Hospital* (Pa.Cmwlth.1993), which held that the negligence of a physician does not automatically give rise to liability of the hospital for corporate negligence. In *Walls*, the court held that expert testimony is required to establish that the conduct of hospital caused harm to the patient. Although it appeared that a physician failed to keep a Wagner fixation device tightened which resulted in a separation of the patient's fracture, the court held that evidence would also be required to establish that the failure of the radiologist to notify the surgeon of the separation was a substantial factor in causing harm. As no causal connection between the hospital and harm was demonstrated, the hospital could not be held liable on a theory of corporate negligence.

Other factors, depending upon state law, also effect the application of the theory of corporate negligence. For instance, Kansas has rejected a theory of corporate negligence that imposes liability on a hospital for failing to select and retain only competent physicians. See *McVay v. Rich* (Kan. App.1993). The Kansas statute, K.S.A. 1992 Supp. 40–3403 (which establishes the Health Care Stabilization Fund), has been interpreted to limit the liability of health care providers and medical facilities who are covered or insured under the fund. It provides that in cases involving an independent contractor, who is qualified under the fund, the hospital "shall have no vicarious liability or responsibility for any injury arising out of the rendering of or failure to render professional services by another health care provider who is also covered by the fund." According to *McVay*, this applies even if a hospital were negligent in the screening of physicians and should have known that a physician was not competent. The apparent policy reason for this statutory provision is the attempt to stabilize liability insurance rates by preventing multiple parties from being liable for any one occurrence.

IV. PATIENT DUMPING

Another basis for direct liability on the part of the hospital is "patient dumping". "Patient dumping" is the practice of refusing to treat, or transferring to another facility, patients who are in an emergency situation and are unable to pay for medical care or do not have insurance coverage. Patients are typically transferred, after minimal stabilization, to a publicly-funded emergency facility which will provide for their care.

Prior to 1988, the obligation of the hospital to provide emergency care arose from statutes governing the licensing of hospitals, and particularly from the standards set by the Joint Commission for Accreditation of Hospitals (JCAH). In *Thompson v. Sun City Community Hospital, Inc.* (Ariz.1984), a mother brought an action for alleged aggravation of her son's injuries resulting from the hospital's transferring him to a local county hospital. The court held that in construing these statutes, public policy prevents a hospital from denying emergency care to a patient without cause. Similarly, the JCAH prohibits the transfer of a patient in need of emergency care for arbitrary reasons such as lack of financial resources. Transfer of a patient in an emergent condition is not appropriate as long as the hospital has the medical resources to adequately handle the problem. Under *Thompson*, a hospital which transfers a patient still requiring emergency care would be liable for damage caused by a transfer to another facility. Furthermore, not only may the hospital be held liable for injury actually *caused* by the transfer or lack of adequate emergency care, but it may also be held liable if its actions increased the *risk* of harm to the patient. An emergency condition is defined as one that requires immediate attention, which condition would be exacerbated if delayed by transfer to another facility.

The duty of hospitals to provide emergency care is now federally mandated as part of the Consolidated Omnibus Budget Reconciliation Act of 1986 (COBRA). This provision is known as the Emergency Medical Treatment and Active Labor Act (EMTALA). It provides that all hospitals which provide emergency room services and receive Medicare funds must follow certain regulations and procedures, including the proper evaluation of patients and treatment to stabilize them prior to any attempt to transfer. See *Coleman v. McCurtain Memorial Medical Management, Inc.* (E.D.Okl.1991). The only exception are those cases where a facility is unable to care for a particular problem and transfers the patient to a better equipped facility. EMTALA's history indicates that the statute was intended to deter hospitals from "dumping" patients who lacked ability to pay. It has been held that the Act applies to all patients. See *Brooker v. Desert Hospital Corp.* (9th Cir.1991).

Coleman makes it clear that the provisions of the EMTALA are only applicable in cases of true emergency. "If a hospital reasonably concludes that no emergency medical condition exists, it can release or transfer a patient without implicating the provisions of the Act." In *Coleman*, a woman admitted to the emergency room was diagnosed with a viral disease. The court found that the hospital was not liable under the Act's anti-dumping provisions, even though the woman was re-admitted two days later with cardiac failure and subsequently died. The court held that situations involving misdiagnosis do not trigger the Act, but instead give rise to an action in negligence or tort law.

In circumstances in which the Act is implicated, there are procedural guidelines that govern the transfer of a patient to another facility. Most importantly, the patient must be medically stabilized. According to the Act: "[t]he term 'stabilized' means, with respect to an emergency medical condition, that no material deterioration of the [patient's] condition is likely, within reasonable medical probability, to result from the transfer of the individual from a facility." Of course, a patient's medical condition does not have to completely alleviated or corrected; it must only be stable enough for transfer to occur. See *Brooker*.

Brooker involved a woman who arrived at an emergency room with a probable heart attack. After admission to the hospital it was determined that she would require cardiac bypass surgery. The assigned surgeon was not to be available for several days, but the woman was deemed clinically stable. Her physician advised transfer to another hospital for more immediate surgery and she suffered a heart attack during the transfer. The court held that the transfer did not violate EMTALA, as the patient's condition, although critical, was nevertheless medically stable.

The circumstances which do warrant the denial of emergency care under the duty created by licensing guidelines and JCAH were articulated in *Thompson*. These defenses include: "(1) the hospital is not obligated (or capable) under its state license to provide the necessary emergency care, (2) there is a valid medical cause to refuse emergency care, (3) there is no true emergency requiring care and thus no emergency care which is medically indicated." *Thompson.*

Of course, a hospital which elects not to treat pursuant to one of these exceptions under EMTALA bears the burden of establishing the exception. Certainly, the status of the hospital's license can be verified. However, whether or not there is a true emergency is usually an issue of fact to be determined by the jury. Similarly, whether there exists valid medical causes to refuse emergency care under EMTALA is also an issue to be ultimately decided by the jury.

CHAPTER NINE

CONTRACT, WARRANTY AND STRICT LIABILITY

I. IN GENERAL: CONTRACT-BASED CLAIMS

When an individual engages the services of a doctor, a contractual relationship arises. The physician makes a promise to the patient that he has the proper qualifications to be a physician, that he will provide the ordinary degree of care, skill and best efforts to render medical services, and in the case of doubt, will use his best professional judgment. The individual promises to pay for the services rendered by the physician. This exchange of promises gives rise to an implied contract in law, the basis for a doctor-patient relationship. In order to recover from a physician on a contract theory, a patient must first establish that the doctor–patient relationship, which gives rise to an implied contract, exists. This implied contract between doctor and patient arises even if formal contract language is not used.

As parties entering into a contract, a physician and a patient are free to expressly contract for services, guarantees and/or results above and beyond what is required to sustain a doctor-patient relationship. It is important to remember, however, that the combination of the uncertainties of medicine and individual anatomical differences make it difficult for doctors to honestly promise or guarantee a certain result.

If a doctor and patient do so contract, and if that service or result is not obtained, the patient then has a cause of action against the physician for breach of contract. *Orozco v. Children's Hosp.* (E.D.Pa.1986), *Murray v. University of Pennsylvania Hospital* (Pa.Super.1985). Some jurisdictions are reluctant to enforce these supposed contracts on grounds of public policy. This reluctance to enforce such agreements stems from a concern that if these contracts are honored, physicians will be hesitant to offer therapeutic reassurances to the patient and will practice "defensive medicine". *Scarzella v. Saxon* (D.C.App.1981), quoting *Sullivan v. O'Connor* (Mass.1973). The argument in favor of enforcing these contracts is that if they are not enforced, there will be no restriction on the promises and assurances of doctors, thus promoting gross exaggeration and misinformation in the attempt to gain business, which will ultimately lead to a breakdown in the confidence of the medical profession.

If a doctor and a patient choose to contract for more than the doctor-patient relationship requires, the problem that frequently arises is whether or not the physician and patient have indeed formed a binding contract for the additional promised objectives. In order to maintain a contract claim against a health provider, a heavy burden of proof will be imposed. One must have "clear proof" that a doctor made a promise/guarantee, separate from the doctor-patient relationship, to prove the existence of an actionable contract. *Van Leeuwan v. Nuzzi* (D.Colo.1993), *Sard v. Hardy* (Md.1977).

In order to meet the burden of clear proof, courts have examined a variety of factors. Generally they will require that the promise be expressly made by the physician to the patient. *Scarzella*. Courts will look to the language used between the parties to determine whether any statement the physician made rises to the level of a guarantee, thus making it a separate contract from the doctor-patient relationship. *Guilmet v. Campbell* (Mich.1971). Ultimately, this is a question for the jury.

Some jurisdictions, in addition to looking at the language used, require "the existence of a contract supported by separate consideration" in order to hold a physician liable for breaching a contract with a patient. *Dorney v. Harris* (D.Colo.1980), *Coleman v. Garrison* (Del.1975).

Other jurisdictions may require proof of separate consideration when the promise is made separate from or after the medical procedure. *Cirafici v. Goffen*, *Sard*. Yet other jurisdictions require no proof of separate consideration where the promise was "an inducement to consent to the treatment". *Depenbrok v. Kaiser Foundation Health Plan*; *Cirafici v. Goffen*.

Finally, some jurisdictions have enacted statutes requiring a separate contract to be in writing and signed by both parties in order to be recognized. Mich.Comp.Laws Ann. § 566.132(g), Del. Code tit.18 § 6851 (1989) (For medical malpractice actions "no claim for breach of contract may be asserted unless such contract is in writing".)

The "clear proof" standard addresses some of the concerns regarding suing physicians on a contract theory. Clear proof allows physicians not to practice defensive medicine and to be able to speak somewhat freely to reassure or lessen the anxiety a patient may experience. The policy considerations behind the clear proof standard are clear. If the burden is too low, physicians would be insurers for all doctor-patients contracts, even if the physician used the requisite care, and it would result in opening the floodgates to this type of litigation and in extending an invitation to meritless claims. If the burden is too great, physicians might freely engage in "puffing"—exaggerating the benefits of a procedure—in order to entire patients to accept their services.

The contract cause of action is entirely separate from the malpractice action despite the fact they both may stem from the same transaction. Malpractice is predicated on negligence (the failure of the physician to exercise the requisite degree of medical skill) and is tortious in nature. The action in contract is based upon failure to perform a specific agreement. *Stewart v. Rudner* (Mich.1957). In malpractice, the damages are for personal injury which include the pain and suffering resulting from the tortious act. In medical malpractice contract actions, standard measures for recovery include "compensatory" or "expectancy" damages which are determined to be an amount that will put the patient in a position as if the contract had never been performed. These damages may include physical and mental suffering. In the alternative, the patient may elect to receive "restitution" damages which are calculated to be an amount corresponding to any benefit given to the defendant physician by the patient in regards to the contractual relationship. *Sullivan,* infra. There is no general agreement among the courts as to how a patient's damages should be calculated and what should be included. It is in the court's discretion to look at the circumstances surrounding the contract to determine what damages may be compensable in a contract action and whether or not compensation for psychological or physical injury is appropriate.

Finally, yet another significant issue distinguishes tort-based claims from contract-based claims in the context of medical injuries. A contract claim usually has a statute of limitations between four and six years, while a tort action generally has a statute of limitations between one and three years, unless contrary legislation has been adopted. In those cases in which the tort statute has expired some plaintiffs have attempted to craft their claim in contract terms.

II. TYPES OF CONTRACT CLAIMS

There are three types of actions that stem from a breach of contract between a doctor and patient:

(1) contracts for a specific result; (2) contracts for specific procedures; and (3) contracts to perform services.

A. CONTRACT FOR SPECIFIC RESULTS

For this type of contract to arise, a physician must contract with the patient that his treatment will produce a specific end. Again, this is difficult to establish because the practice of medicine has many attendant uncertainties and human anatomy is unique to each individual. *Sullivan v. O'Connor* (Mass.1973). If such a contract has been made and the specific results do not follow, the patient has a potential contract claim against the physician.

One way to determine whether or not a contract for specific results has been made is exemplified in *Guilmet v. Campbell* (Mich.1971). In *Guilmet*, the patient suffered from a peptic ulcer and consulted a physician who recommended a vagotomy (nerve severing surgery) to remedy the problem. The doctor told the patient that this surgery would take care of the problem, that the operation was very simple and that the patient would be out of work for no more than four weeks. The patient underwent an unsuccessful vagotomy which not only required three more operations to correct the problem, but resulted in a series of infections and possible faulty blood transfusions. The issue of whether a contract existed was resolved by the jury based solely on the testimonial evidence presented by the doctor and the patient; there was no writing memorializing the alleged contract and no additional consideration had been provided. The jury found that the doctor was not negligent but awarded the patient damages upon a determination that the doctor had breached the parties' contract for specific results.

Contrast *Guilmet* with *Clevenger v. Haling* (Mass. 1979). In *Clevenger*, a patient, after having a tubal ligation in order to prevent future pregnancies, became pregnant and sued doctor for breach of contract for a specific result. In establishing whether the doctor was liable for failure to deliver the promised result, the court closely examined exactly what the doctor told the patient to determine whether or not the parties had entered into a specific contract. In *Clevenger*, using the clear proof standard, recovery was denied against the doctor for breach of contract for a specific result. The court determined that the doctor's statements to the patient that the procedure was a "permanent thing" and "you are not going to have any more children after this operation" did not create a contract between the parties. Since the doctor did not use words promissory in nature (i.e. "I promise you will not have anymore children"), the patient's claim for breach of contract failed.

It is difficult to determine whether or not a contract for specific results can be proved based only on oral testimony. For example, a doctor's statement that a certain procedure would "please" the patient or enhance the patient's appearance might rise to the level of a guarantee in some courts but not in others.

In *Sullivan v. O'Connor* (Mass.1973), the patient, a well-known professional entertainer, agreed to surgery performed by the defendant doctor upon his promise "to perform plastic surgery on her nose and thereby enhance her beauty and improve her appearance." The surgery, in fact, disfigured the patient's nose and caused her to suffer physical and mental pain. The court determined that an express contract did exist between the doctor and the patient and that the patient was entitled to damages. However, in *Rosenblum v. Cherner* (D.C.App.1966), the court held that a dentist who told his patient that the work he would perform on the patient would "please her to her personal satisfaction", was determined not to create a contract between the physician and patient.

As mentioned above, to obtain consistency and predictability among medical malpractice cases alleging contract claims, courts have imposed certain standards, and even some states have enacted specific legislation to promote uniformity of results. Such legislation usually mandates that either a writing is required or there must be evidence of additional consideration in order to prevail on a contract theory. The intent is to obviate the problem that results when an express warranty is made. See *Hawkins v. McGee* (N.H.1929), where defendant doctor expressly promised to make patient's injured hand into a good or perfect hand and in fact made patient's hand worse. The doctor was liable in contract to the patient for the value of a good or perfect hand.

B. SPECIFIC PROCEDURES

An action in contract may also arise if a physician contracts with the patient to use a specific procedure and does not use that particular procedure or uses another which he has not contracted to perform.

In *Stewart v. Rudner* (Mich.1957), a woman explicitly contracted with her doctor to deliver her baby by cesarean section as she had had two previous stillbirths and feared for her own physical safety as well as that of her in-utero child. In *Stewart*, as each and every time the patient met with the doctor over the course of her pregnancy the cesarean procedure was discussed, there was no dispute as to the existence of a contract. At the time of delivery, however, another physician was on duty and the child was delivered vaginally, and was stillborn. The original doctor with whom the agreement was made was held liable for breaching the contract for a specific procedure.

A cause of action for breach of contract may also arise from contracted non-medical duties as well as from the failure to render health care. For example, in *Chew v. Paul D. Meyer, M.D., P.A.* (Md.App. 1987), the patient's employer required all employees who missed work to produce a written explanation of their absence within fifteen days of the day missed. The patient underwent surgery and explained his employer's requirement to the doctor. There is no claim that the surgery was not successful in any manner. The patient provided the doctor with his employer's forms to be completed to verify the reason for the patient's absence from work and stressed the importance of the forms. The doctor failed to complete the forms in a timely manner and the patient was fired. The court denied summary judgment, holding that a jury could find that the doctor had a contractual obligation to the patient. Furthermore, the jury could also find not only "... contractual privity [but] that [such] privity would carry with it a concomitant tort duty."

C. CONTRACTS TO PERFORM SERVICES

When a patient and a doctor specifically contract that a particular physician will perform the contracted for services, and the physician does not do so, the patient may recover in a breach of contract action. In these actions, usually the doctor does not treat the patient and engages a substitute physician (or resident) to perform the services. In *Alexandridis v. Jewett* (1st Cir.1968), a woman contracted with a highly competent and experienced doctor to deliver her baby. The doctor and patient contracted that if this doctor was not available at the time of the patient's delivery, his equally qualified partner would perform the services required. The delivery, however, was performed by a first-year resident rather than the covering doctor. The patient, as a result of delivery, suffered rectal incontinence. The court held that even though the resident was not negligent, there was a breach of contract for which the plaintiff could recover. *Alexan-*

dridis seems to hold that even if the delivery had been performed competently by a more qualified and experienced physician, the doctor with whom the patient had contracted would still be liable for a breach of contract, although not for negligence. Once again, in order to successfully recover, the patient must prove by clear proof that there existed a specific contract with a physician for something more than professional services.

II. PRODUCT LIABILITY

Hospitals and physicians use and provide to patients products that are manufactured by others. The hospital's and physician's responsibilities attendant to the use of such products include using such products correctly and warning patients about possible risks and side effects of the product selected.

In *Karibjanian v. Thomas Jefferson University Hospital* (E.D.Pa.1989), a widow alleged that her husband's death was caused by an injection of thorium dioxide administered by an agent of the defendant hospital. The widow alleged that the injection should not have been administered, that this product was inherently unsafe and that the defendant hospital knew or should have known it to be so. The widow's claim relied upon § 402A of the Restatement (Second) of Torts which states in part:

"(1) One who sells any product in a defective condition unreasonably dangerous to the user or consumer ... is subject to liability ... if (a) the seller is engaged in the business of selling such a product...."

The defendant hospital contended that it was not in the "business of selling" thorium dioxide and instead, merely provided its services to the widow's decedent. The court held that as long as a hospital *regularly* supplies such a product to its patients, even if incidental to the services provided by the hospital, the hospital may be held liable under § 402A as § 402A does not distinguish between a supplier of goods who also supplies services and a supplier who only supplies goods. In *Karibjanian*, the plaintiff was allowed to proceed with her claim against the hospital, and thus would given the opportunity to present evidence that the thorium dioxide came from the defendant hospital's inventory, that the hospital supplied it to plaintiff's decedent and that the hospital regularly supplied this injection and product to other patients.

In most cases, prior to using or administering potentially dangerous products, a physician has a duty to warn patients about the risks and side effects associated with the product to be used. An example of the duty of the physician to warn patients about possible risks and side effects with regard to products manufactured by others is illustrated in *Tresemer v. Barke* (Cal.App.1978). In *Tresemer*, the plaintiff alleged that the defendant doctor breached his duty to warn her of the dangers of the Dalkon Shield when, subsequent to its insertion, he obtained knowledge of the dangers and did not notify the plaintiff. As a general rule, a defendant owes a duty of care to all persons who are foreseeably endangered by his conduct. *Dillon v. Legg* (Cal.1968). The real question was whether it was the physician or the manufacturer who was responsible for providing the subsequent information to the patient. In assessing the manufacturer's liability, courts have consistently held that a manufacturer is not liable where the physician using the manufacturer's product has been made sufficiently aware of the risks associated with that product. *Wooten v. Johnson & Johnson Products, Inc.* (N.D.Ill.1986).

Tresemer states that the duty of the manufacturer to adequately warn is discharged by its warning of possible and actual dangers to the physicians as "it would be virtually impossible for a manufacturer to comply with the duty of direct warning, as there is no sure way to reach the patient." Once a physician is adequately informed by the manufacturer of the actual and possible dangers of a product, the physician "acts as a learned intermediary between the patient and the . . . manufacturer, thus breaking the chain of liability." *Kirk v. Michael Reese Hospital and Medical Center* (Ill.1987). *Tresemer* holds that an action for failure to warn the patient may be maintained against the physician due to the continuing confidential relationship between the physician and patient and the fact that the danger arose from that relationship.

III. STRICT LIABILITY

Strict liability has yet to be applied to a physician with regard to his duties to a patient, although in scattered cases plaintiff have attempted to hold the physician liable on a such a theory. In *Hoven v. Kelble* (Wis.1977), a plaintiff alleged strict liability against the defendant doctor on the basis that he was indeed a seller in the business of selling medical services and that the defective services rendered by defendant doctor were the cause of plaintiff's damages. *Hoven,* like *Karibjanian,* relies upon the Restatement (Second) of Torts § 402A to determine whether strict liability may be extended to the defendant for personal injuries occurring during the delivery of medical services. *Hoven* acknowledged that the § 402A strict liability test had not been applied beyond the sale of a defective and dangerous product; indeed, it had never been applied on the basis of medical services. The court did discuss the pros and cons of extending strict liability to the professional services of physicians. It reasoned that doctors contract with patients to provide treatment in a non-negligent manner, and that a patient cannot deem a doctor's treatment to be defective merely because he is not cured. Since the medical profession is not exact and a doctor is only required to provide treatment commensurate with the state of medical science, there is likely no social benefit in holding a physician strictly liable for his professional practices. To hold a physician strictly liable may make doctors reluctant to treat patients with certain conditions.

Of course, the consumer of these services relies upon the skill and information of the physician, and the hospital and/or doctor is in a better position than the patient to ensure safe and effective treatment. Furthermore, the imposition of strict liability may be a strong deterrent to negligence as it encourages knowledge and safety. Nevertheless, the court concluded that society needs medical services and it is essential for these services to be readily available. The imposition of strict liability would likely increase the cost for those services and hinder much needed medical science advances. Having society's best interest and its need for medical services in mind, the court refused to impose strict liability upon physicians and hospitals under § 402A due to the "unknown costs and inability to assess the results" attendant with such a extension. The court noted, however, the ever-changing aspect of tort liability and recognized the possibility of applying strict liability in the future.

CHAPTER TEN

REFORMING THE LITIGATION SYSTEM

I. IN GENERAL: COST VS. QUALITY

Legislation and case law regarding the quality of and access to medical care may be more effective in addressing the medical malpractice crisis and reform of the litigation system than has previously been recognized. The primary objective of utilization review of health care resources and tort reform of malpractice cases has been the containment of health care costs. As insurance liability premiums rise, the costs are passed on to consumers. Additionally, the increase in malpractice litigation and the size of the awards has forced many physicians to practice "defensive medicine", i.e., excessive tests and procedures are ordered in an effort to avoid any possible oversight in the diagnosis and treatment of the patient. In response, health care insurers have instituted utilization review procedures in order to determine whether particular health care procedures should be "allowed", i.e., paid for by the insurance carriers.

At the same time, licensing, accreditation, medical standards and other requirements for continuous quality improvement demand a certain level of care. These same standards are often used to determine the existence of a duty to the patient, as well as the level of care for evaluating a claim of negligence.

What seems to result is conflicting goals of the health care delivery system: cost containment (which limits the amount of resources utilized), and quality control (which demands a certain level of care, largely ignoring cost). The tension between these competing goals results in the development of a standard of care that recognizes limited medical resources and limited insurance coverage along with a tort system unwilling to accommodate such cost considerations. The focus on tort reform has been to reduce the numbers of cases that require judicial resources (for example, by requiring mandatory arbitration) and to limit the awards that litigation can yield by, for example, putting caps on recoveries. See Jonathan J. Frankel, Medical Malpractice Law and Health Care Cost Containment: Lessons For Reformers From The Clash of Cultures, 103 Yale L.J. 1297, (1994).

The challenge is evident: any effort at reform of the tort system must take into consideration the changing medical environment and shared decision making authority which has resulted from changes in health care delivery. Specifically, physicians are no longer the sole managers of patient care. They share this responsibility with hospital administrators, third party payers and ultimately utilization review boards. Changes in decision making authority clearly has an impact on the nature of care provided, although the duty owed to the patient has not necessarily been altered accordingly. Indeed, many would argue that it is undesirable to modify the duty and/or standard of care legally required, since to do so would likely compromise patient welfare.

A. UTILIZATION REVIEW AND ACCESS TO CARE

Utilization review is a process used to determine whether certain care provided to a patient is medically necessary and thus reimbursable. Utilization review can be prospective or retrospective. The latter process, whereby the patient record is reviewed after the care has been provided, is generally used pursuant to federally mandated guidelines for reimbursement under Medicare and for accreditation by the Joint Commission for Accreditation of Hospitals (JCAH). Reimbursement to health care providers is often adjusted according to a certain rate which is set in accordance with the standard applicable to the procedure. If the procedure is ultimately deemed unnecessary, reimbursement may be withheld entirely. The federal organization which reviews care to determine eligibility for coverage under Medicare and Medicaid is the Peer Review Organization (PRO) which is established pursuant to 42 U.S.C.A. § 1320c, et seq., Peer Review Improvement Act and its amendments.

Prospective utilization review calls for review of a case before care is given. The insurance company's utilization agent determines whether certain care is authorized as medically necessary and therefore will be reimbursed. This is a common reimbursement scheme used by health maintenance organizations. See *Wickline v. State of California* (Cal.App.1986).

In *Wickline*, a woman required vascular surgery to improve blood circulation in both of her legs. The state utilization organization, Medi–Cal, authorized ten days of in-patient care for the procedure. After surgery, the patient developed complications which required further hospitalization. In view of her "stormy" recovery, the surgeon requested an eight day extension of her hospital stay beyond that already authorized by Medi–Cal. Medi–Cal approved only four days of the eight day extension requested by the physician. The patient remained in the hospital for four days and was then discharged. At home, she developed severe complications including an infection at the surgical site and blood clots. The patient subsequently required amputation of her leg. After being re-hospitalized nine days after discharge, she alleged that her premature discharge caused the severity of the complications. According to her complaint, if she had been permitted to remain in the hospital, the complications would have been detected earlier in time to save her leg.

The California Court of Appeals declined to find liability on behalf of Medi–Cal since there was no evidence that the physician exhausted his option to keep the patient hospitalized by re-contacting Medi–Cal at the end of the four days to request continued care. Nevertheless, the court did establish that an organization performing utilization review owes a duty of care to the patient:

> "The patient who requires treatment and who is harmed when care which should be provided is not provided should recover for the injuries suffered from all those responsible for the deprivation of such care, including, when appropriate, health care payers."

Unreasonable disregard of *appeals* of non-coverage decisions may qualify as an "appropriate trigger of liability".

The standard applied in *Wickline* may differ in the private insurance sector where the duty of care is governed by the insurance contract. Nevertheless, if the contract establishes a duty, utilization review decisions can trigger liability if they result in injury to a patient. In *Wilson v. Blue Cross of So. California* (Cal.App.1990), a psychiatric patient committed suicide after being discharged from a hospital. The agent responsible for the utilization review decisions refused to authorize additional inpatient treatment, even though the treating physician requested 3–4 weeks of further hospital care. The court held that the utilization review board could be held at least partially liable if its determination was negligent and was a substantial factor in bringing about the suicide.

Corcoran v. United Healthcare, Inc. (5th Cir.1992) also recognized that utilization review decisions substantially affect treatment decisions, as patients are likely to choose that which is authorized or covered by the plan.   In *Corchoran*, a pregnant woman agreed to be discharged to home nursing when her HMO would not authorize in-patient coverage.   She ultimately lost her 32–week fetus which went into fetal distress during the absence of the nurse.   No actual determination about liability was made, however, as it was determined that the claim was preempted by the Employee Retirement Income Security Act (ERISA).   See Peter H. Mihaly, Health Care Utilization Review: Potential Exposures to Negligence Liability, 52 Ohio St. L.J. 1289 (1991).

B.   PEER REVIEW AND MEDICAL MALPRACTICE LITIGATION

Efforts of the medical community to improve the quality and delivery of health care have resulted in both voluntary and statutorily mandated review of services by means of peer review or quality assessment procedures.   As a consequence, the issue has arisen as to the discoverability of information compiled by peer review committees in the course of their proceedings.   Typically such discovery is sought by a medical malpractice plaintiff who seeks to determine whether a hospital knew that its physician was not competent to perform a certain procedure, or whether a subsequent inquiry into the particular incident yielded any significant (or helpful) findings.

Most recent cases recognize the confidentiality of certain peer review materials.   However, any immunity from discovery is likely to depend upon the type of peer review organization or quality assurance committee which has generated the information.   A peer review organization (PRO) reviews care for eligibility under federal reimbursement programs such as Medicare.   A utilization review committee, in contrast, performs a broader function.   Typically it is a committee which is created to determine necessity of care (and thus coverage). Utilization review is now common in state and private insurance programs.   A type of "peer review" may also be performed by those committees which evaluate quality assurance, "continuous quality improvement", staff credentials and similar programs.   See *Todd v. So. Jersey Hospital System* (D.N.J.1993).   Whether the documents generated by such "peer review" groups is protected from discovery is dependent upon both the type of committee that generates the information and any statutory provisions concerning confidentiality.

Federal protection of confidentiality of documents for PROs is provided by the Peer Review Improvement Act.   A leading judicial decision in this area is *General Care Corp. v. Mid–South Foundation for Medical Care, Inc.* (W.D.Tenn. 1991).   The court held that information compiled by a PRO is presumed to be confidential and thus the hospital was not required to disclose it.   *Todd*, supra, supported this decision, holding that the Peer Review Improvement Act protected from discovery documents that were collected and generated by the PRO while performing its statutorily defined functions.   Nevertheless, *Todd* also qualified its holding by stating that these same documents would be discoverable if they could be independently obtained from another committee or department. See *Todd*. In *Chandra v. Sprinkle* (Mo.1984), by contrast, a Missouri court held that no peer review privilege existed to protect the discovery of factual information compiled by an "Ad Hoc Committee" which was appointed by the hospital to investigate the care of an infant who suffered respiratory arrest. The court refused to recognize any self-evaluation privilege in the absence of a statute, and issued an order compelling discovery, despite public policy concerns that confidentiality of such documents is necessary to maintain an effective evaluation program. In contrast to *Chandre,* most courts do hold that peer review documents should be protected from discovery, particularly if so ordered by statute. See *Morse v. Gerity* (D.Conn.1981).

Protection of documents generated by utilization review committees and other such groups is governed primarily by state statute. Virtually all such statutes provide protection of committee members from personal liability for their participation as peer review members. Such protection is not necessarily provided, however, for information generated by other types of groups. This varies among states, and is governed by local statute.

In those cases where peer review or quality control groups are not covered by statute, a state may recognize such protection as a "critical self-analysis" privilege at common law. "The purpose of this privilege is to encourage self-evaluation and the benefits that may flow therefrom, and to avoid the chilling effect upon such self-analysis which would result from complete disclosure." *Todd*. Such privileges are generally not absolute and can be overridden by a showing that the need for production of documents outweighs the public interest in confidentiality. Usually a court will balance the availability of the information from other sources, the harm that non-disclosure will cause, and any possible prejudice to the organization's investigation. In *Todd*, the court held that the patient's need for information regarding alleged negligent obstetrical care was sufficient to overcome the critical self-analysis privilege. Consequently, it ordered production of certain quality assurance documents, even though materials generated specifically by "Utilization Review" were protected by statute and not subject to discovery.

Such privileges from discovery recognize the inherent conflict between improving quality of care by candid review procedures and assisting an injured plaintiff in proving his claim of negligence. The goal of minimizing costs of health care litigation may eventually affect the discoverability of opinions or reports prepared by peer review or utilization review organizations.

II. ACCESSIBILITY, QUALITY, AND AFFORDABILITY

Reform of the litigation system in the 1990s attempts to address several concerns. One is accessi-

bility of health care, as escalating costs of malpractice liability insurance have driven physicians out of
certain practice areas.   Another is quality of care,
as physicians have been forced to practice defensive
medicine, which thereby limits the overall resources
for adequate care.   A third is affordability, since
escalating costs of health care are inevitably passed
on to consumers.

Reform of the litigation system has taken the
form of encouraging alternative dispute resolution
including arbitration, mediation and early settlement, as well as the screening of spurious claims.
A number of states have imposed limitations on
contingent fee arrangements between the attorney
and client so that more of the award goes to the
injured plaintiff.   Some states have eliminated the
collateral source rule which otherwise precludes the
plaintiff from recovering from both the tortfeasor
and a collateral source, such as insurance.   Some
jurisdictions now permit allocation of liability
among tortfeasors and may allow claims under theories such as enterprise liability.   A number of
jurisdictions have imposed limitations on the total
amount of damages that can be awarded.   Some
have attempted to abolish joint and several liability.
Some states have reduced litigation by shortening
the applicable statute of limitations for medical
malpractice claims.   See Marshall B. Kapp, Medical
Malpractice Reform as Part of Health Care Reform,
1994 Version, 68 May FLBJ 28 (1994).   Most of
these legislative efforts have survived constitutional
challenges.

Another difficulty with reforming the health care delivery system is that there is little agreement as to how to evaluate the success of various measures. The only consensus has been that statutory limitations on damages have been effective, assuming, of course, that effectiveness is measured by a reduction in the frequency and severity of claims and by lower insurance premiums. *Kapp,* supra.

A. AVAILABILITY OF MALPRACTICE INSURANCE

The initial concern about the large number of malpractice claims and the size of the awards was that it would affect the availability of medical care by forcing physicians to practice defensive medicine. Another major concern has been the effect of such awards on the availability of affordable malpractice insurance to health care professionals, particularly the physician.   As successful claims increased, many malpractice insurers suffered severe losses and either withdrew from the market or increased their premiums dramatically.   See *Meier v. Anderson* (E.D.Pa.1988).   Many states responded with the legislative efforts discussed earlier aimed at limiting or reallocating such losses.

The medical community (and others to whom the losses have shifted) has also responded.   One approach has been to attack the legislation on constitutional grounds.   In *Meier,* a physician challenged the Pennsylvania tort reform scheme which both limited the liability of the insurer and reallocated the losses. Specifically, the act required health care providers to contribute to a fund from which victims of malpractice could collect their awards if the awards were in excess of the limits of the insurance to ensure that they received adequate compensation. The Act was constitutionally challenged on the basis that the right to practice one's profession is protected by both the due process and the equal protection clause of the fourteenth amendment. Such legislation was alleged to have potential economic effects on that right. The court held that the right at issue was not a fundamental right "explicitly or implicitly guaranteed by the Constitution", and therefore not worthy of special protection. Therefore, any challenge to the law would be subject to the rational basis standard, and the law would stand if there was a rational basis for concluding that the law serves a legitimate governmental interest. In denying that the law was unconstitutional, the court noted that the "state has a legitimate state interest in regulating the practice of medicine and assuring the availability of medical malpractice insurance, and can enact nonarbitrary legislation to that end without violating substantive due process."

The *Meier* court also rejected the defendant's equal protection challenge alleging that the Act was underinclusive as it targeted only medical doctors and not other professionals such as chiropractors. It also rejected the argument that law was overinclusive as it required all doctors to pay into the fund regardless of their past claims history. These provisions were held to be rationally related to the goals of the Act which was to increase the availability of malpractice insurance. The "rational basis" standard makes it difficult to challenge such legislation on constitutional grounds.

B.   INSURER'S DUTY TO DEFEND AND INDEMNIFY AND SETTLE

The insurer's duty to defend, indemnify and even settle (if practical) is important both to the interests of the professional, who may be liable for a substantial award, and to the injured party, who seeks just and timely compensation. The obligation of an insurer to defend its insured is broader than the duty of indemnity.

In *Snyder v. National Union Fire Insurance Co.* (S.D.N.Y.1988), the court held that to trigger the duty to defend, the "plaintiff need merely to show that her complaint brings the claim within the coverage of the policy." The pleadings must allege actions and injury that are within the terms of the policy. The duty to defend arises whether or not ultimate liability will be proved. A North Carolina court referred to this as the "comparison test", which involves comparing the allegations of the complaint side-by-side with the particular terms of the policy to determine if the duty to defend arises. If so, the insurance company is obligated to provide a defense regardless of the ultimate disposition of the case. See *St. Paul Fire and Marine Ins. Co. v. Vigilant Ins. Co.* (M.D.N.C.1989). In *St. Paul*, a duty to defend was held to exist even though a second insurance company had assumed coverage during the latter part of the doctor-patient relationship.

In *Snyder*, the plaintiff alleged both civil liability for malpractice and criminal liability for assault and sexual abuse. The issue arose as to whether the insurer's duty to defend was negated by the criminal allegations (and ultimate conviction of the physician) as the policy contained an exclusion of coverage for injury resulting from criminal acts. The court held that in order for an insurance company to avoid an obligation to defend, it must show the allegations are *entirely* within the exclusions of the policy. See *Snyder*, supra.

Indemnification, however, is another story. Whether the insurer must pay on a claim will depend upon the liability of the insured and, if an exclusion applies, upon whether the findings by the court bring the case within that policy's exclusion. In *Snyder,* the plaintiff was required to show both (a) that there was no intent to cause injury and (b) that the injury did not arise from the criminal acts of alleged sexual abuse. If the injury did result from criminal acts, the insurer would be entitled to disclaim coverage under the policy.

Whether an insurance company is defending or settling claims against its insured, it owes "a duty to act in good faith and without negligence." *Insurance Company of North America v. Medical Protective Co.* (10th Cir.1985). In *Brown v. Guarantee*

Co. (Cal.App.1957), the court suggested several factors to aid in a determination of "bad faith", although such factors may of course vary among courts. These include:

> "1) the strength of the insured claimant's case on the issue of liability and damages; 2) attempts by the insurer to induce the insured to contribute to a settlement; 3) failure of the insurer to properly investigate the circumstances so as to ascertain the evidence against the insured; 4) the insurer's rejection of advice of its own attorney or agent; 5) failure of the insurer to inform the insured of a compromise offer; 6) the amount of financial risk to which each party is exposed in the event of a refusal to settle; 7) the fault of the insured in inducing the insurer's rejection of a compromise offer by misleading it as to the facts; and 8) any other factors tending to establish or negate bad faith on the part of the insurer."

The insurer also has a duty to keep the physician informed of all settlement negotiations, and to act in good faith, without negligence in efforts to effect a settlement. This duty remains in effect whether or not the insured is willing to consent to any settlement.

C. SCREENING OF SPURIOUS CLAIMS

Another legislative response to the rising number of malpractice claims has been establishing mechanisms for screening spurious claims. The goal of such legislation is to increase the availability of malpractice insurance and health care by discouraging unwarranted claims, and to avoid the expense of frivolous litigation which wastes judicial and medical resources. This type of legislation is frequently challenged constitutionally, on the basis that it violates equal protection and due process of law, and/or that it interferes with access to the court system and the right of trial by jury. As new legislation is being tailored to address these concerns, and as courts primarily have employed a "rational basis" level of review when evaluating these claims, the majority of the legislative reforms have been able to withstand constitutional scrutiny. Specifically, most measures have been found to be rationally or reasonably related to the goals of reducing the costs associated with large numbers of medical malpractice claims.

Whether a particular legislative scheme will survive a constitutional challenge depends upon the method of screening, and the effect of the screen, i.e., under what conditions a plaintiff may gain access to the courts after being "screened out" on a claim that was held to lack merit. See *Keyes v. Humana Hospital Alaska, Inc.* (Alaska 1988). The types of screening measures vary among jurisdictions. Some states require that prior to litigation being commenced, a mediation process be made available to the litigants. Other states require screening of all claims prior to litigation by an expert panel or a judicial tribunal. The findings of such a panel or tribunal are used to evaluate the merit of the case, and may be admissible in the litigation which follows. See *Blood v. Lea* (Mass. 1988); *Aldana v. Holub* (Fla.1980).

Constitutional claims that the screening process violates equal protection have been based primarily on the allegation that a malpractice litigant is treated differently from other tort litigants, as the screening process requires a malpractice claimant to undergo an additional step in the judicial process not required of other tort litigants. Once again, since the malpractice litigant does not belong to a suspect class in need of any special protection, there only need be a rational basis for the legislation. Today, most screening mechanisms generally survive the equal protection arguments. See *Keyes*.

Screening legislation has also been challenged on due process grounds. The typical argument is that such screening mechanisms violate the plaintiff's right to access to the courts and potentially the right to trial by jury, particularly if the screen is mandatory. The level of due process protection afforded to the plaintiff for access to the courts depends upon the substantive claim. Again, no special due process protection is afforded to malpractice litigants since the right they assert is not entitled to special protection. Absent the claim of a fundamental right, courts have held that access to the courts may be delayed, as long as there is a rational basis for doing so. Reducing unnecessary costs of malpractice litigation has been held to constitute a rational reason for delay. *Keyes*.

The right to trial by jury has also been held not to be compromised where the opinion of the review panel serves merely as evidence or as a "rebuttable presumption" in the jury trial which follows.   In such a case, the same evidence and arguments may be presented to the jury to rebut the panel's opinion.   Screening mechanisms which may compromise the right to trial by jury typically involve schemes which give the panels original jurisdiction.   In practice, this results in repeated delays of the case so that the right to trial by jury may be difficult to exercise. *Keyes.*   In *Keyes*, however, the maximum possible delay was eighty days, and the court held that the right to trial by jury was not unreasonably affected.   On the other hand, screening mechanisms which make determinations as to liability and damages, or which serve as the sole basis for judgment, may violate the right to a jury trial by conferring judicial powers inappropriately.   See *Keyes*; *Feinstein v. Mass. General Hospital* (D.Mass.1979).

Objections based upon substantive due process grounds to medical review panels or screening tribunals have been uniformly rejected.   The courts have found "[t]he review procedure to be a reasonable legislative response to a perceived crisis in medical malpractice insurance rates, a means of assuring the availability of malpractice insurance coverage at reasonable rates and of improving the availability and reducing the cost of medical care in general, by attempting to eliminate frivolous malpractice claims and encourage settlement of meritorious ones."   See *Keyes*.

Procedural due process safeguards are not compromised if the litigant is provided a full opportunity to present his case at trial. Procedural due process rights are also protected where the decisions of the screening panels or tribunals are subject to appeal. The function of such review panels is generally to evaluate the claim to determine whether there is sufficient evidence to raise a legitimate question of liability. It has been held that the tribunal should use the same standard as a judge would use in ruling on a motion for directed verdict. The function of the tribunal is to evaluate the sufficiency, not the weight, of the evidence. See *Blood v. Lea* (Mass.1988). Typically state screening requirements are also applicable in federal courts in diversity actions. See *Feinstein*; *Woods v. Holy Cross Hospital* (5th Cir.1979). The federal court in *Seck by Seck v. Hamrang* (S.D.N.Y.1987), however, held to the contrary on the basis that the screening process amounted to a pretrial procedure that was not required in a federal court. *Seck by Seck* commented that to require compliance with the screening mechanisms of the state would conflict with the broad procedural powers of federal courts.

While most state screening procedures have been carefully tailored to avoid constitutional infirmity, some constitutional challenges have been successful. In *Aldana v. Holub* (Fla.1980), the mediation procedure included a mandatory ten-month limitation period which provided that if the process was not completed within the ten month period, for *any* reason, (including unavailability of space on court dockets), the right was denied. The court held that the legislature scheme violated due process in that its rigid requirements concerning the time limits was arbitrary and capricious. The court commented that allowing extensions to the time limits would not correct the constitutional problem since the law itself constituted a denial of access to the courts.

An alternative to screening panels used in some courts is the "certificate of merit" requirement. Such legislation typically requires that the plaintiff's attorney certify that he has consulted with a knowledgeable health professional in the same specialty as the defendant who has reviewed the case and issued a written report. The health professional must conclude that there are reasonable grounds for filing the action, and the report must be filed with an affidavit or certification by plaintiff's attorney. See e.g. Ill. Rev. Stat., Chap. 110. Some courts have held such legislation to be constitutional, while others have held that it unconstitutionally delegates judicial power to non-judicial persons, in derogation of separation of powers doctrine.

III. CHANGING THE LITIGATION SYSTEM

A. ARBITRATION

Another constitutionally sound avenue for deterring litigation is an agreement to arbitrate executed prior to treatment. (The decision to arbitrate may, of course, be made voluntarily by both parties at the time of litigation.)   In *Morris v. Metriyakool* (Mich. 1984), a patient was offered an arbitration option on her admission form at the time she entered the hospital.   The form complied with Michigan law which required that the option be stated on the form in large, boldface type immediately above the patient's signature.   It had to be clear that the arbitration provision was optional and further, it had to be revocable within sixty (60) days after patient's the discharge.   The court held that the Michigan law which provided arbitration by a three member panel "did not deprive patients of a fair and impartial decision maker in violation of their due process rights."   Furthermore, such agreements did not constitute contracts of adhesion.

Houk v. Furman (D.Me.1985) concerned the constitutionality of yet another legislative scheme: Maine's requirement that the plaintiff submit a 90–day "pre-litigation notice" which was intended to encourage settlement or non-judicial resolution of malpractice actions.   The statute was held not to violate equal protection or due process protections, even though non-compliance with the statute resulted in the denial of recovery.   The court also held that the notice provision applied in federal court diversity actions as well as in state claims. Using the rational basis standard of review, *Houk* held that the law had a rational relationship to the purpose of encouraging settlement of claims and of disposing of claims through alternative dispute resolution.   The court also held that although non-compliance could bar recovery, it was not an unduly burdensome requirement that would offend due process requirements.

B.   CAPS ON MALPRACTICE AWARDS

Another legislative tool used to respond to the large number of malpractice cases and the rise in health care costs is statutory caps on damages awarded by the courts.   In some cases overall caps are imposed; in others only certain types of damages such as noneconomic loss/recovery are limited. Other legislation, such as allowing installment payments on future damages, has been enacted to regulate the manner in which damages are paid.   In *Etheridge v. Medical Center Hospitals* (Va.1989), the jury returned a verdict in the amount of $2,750,000.00 against two defendants whose negligence resulted in brain damage and paralysis of the plaintiff.   In accordance with Virginia's statutory recovery limit, the trial court reduced the verdict to $750,000.00 and the plaintiff challenged the constitutionality of the statute.   The plaintiff alleged privacy violations on the basis that the statutory cap "preordains the result of the hearing" as well as an equal protection violation as malpractice plaintiffs are treated differently form other tort victims.   A separation of powers claim was also made on the basis that caps serve to interfere "with the power of the court to enforce its own judgments."   The court rejected all such claims holding that the statutory scheme was a reasonable exercise of legitimate goals.

Once again, as malpractice litigants are not designated as a suspect class and no fundamental right has been identified regarding these claims, the courts on both the federal and state level generally apply a "rational basis" level of review. In most cases the courts are able to identify a reasonable basis for the legislature to conclude that imposing caps on damage awards promotes the legitimate state objective of reducing the cost of malpractice. The caps on malpractice awards appear to be applicable in both state and federal actions. See *Hoffman v. United States* (9th Cir.1985); *Adams v. Children's Mercy Hospital* (Mo.1992); *Keeton v. Mansfield Obstetrics and Gynecology Assoc., Inc.* (N.D.Ohio 1981).

Limitations on damage awards have also been claimed to compromise the plaintiff's right to trial by jury. This approach has also not been very successful. As explained in *Adams v. Childrens Mercy Hospital* (Mo.1992), the jury has no substantive right to determine damages, despite the fact that the primary role of the jury is fact-finding, which includes determining an assessment of damages. Nevertheless, it is the function of the court to apply the substantive law to the fact finding process which may legitimately include the application of damage limitations. See *Adams*. Thus it has been held that the role of the jury is to determine or assess the damages, not to dictate the consequences of that determination. See *Etheridge v. Medical Center Hospitals* (Va.1989).

The reasoning in *Etheridge* and similar opinions was criticized in *Keeton v. Mansfield Obstetrics and Gynecology Assoc., Inc.* (N.D.Ohio 1981). *Keeton* questioned the rationale that controlling the cost of malpractice insurance would promote the availability of health care services. The court in *Keeton* held that the legislative goal was to shift the risk of medical malpractice from the provider to the patient (who is least able to afford it) by limiting the patient's ability to obtain full compensation for the negligence. *Keeton* agreed, however, that the measures were not unconstitutional:

> "Although this Court has very seriously questioned the reasoning behind this legislation and is very dissatisfied with its effect (placing the burden of paying for the negligence of health care providers on those least able to afford it—the seriously injured plaintiff), the Court also recognizes that its only function is to determine whether the challenged legislation is a reasonable exertion of governmental authority or whether the legislation is shown to be arbitrary and capricious."

C. CAPS ON ATTORNEY'S FEES

As an alternative to limiting the amount of awards in malpractice claims, some legislation limits the amount of the legal fee that the attorney may receive pursuant to a contingency fee agreement. Such limitations have also not been found to violate equal protection, due process, or the separation of powers doctrine. See *Roa v. Lodi Medical Group, Inc.* (Cal.1985). In *Roa*, a due process violation was claimed on the basis that the limitation interfered with the right to obtain counsel. The plaintiff argued that if fees were too low, it might be impossible to obtain counsel at all, and that less incentive would exist for an attorney to pursue additional damages. The court rejected this argument, citing a long history of cases establishing the validity of regulating attorney fees. Indeed, limitation of fees may prevent attorney's from fabricating unjust claims in order to collect such fees. In addition, limitations may protect legitimate plaintiffs from extortion by unscrupulous attorneys.

Roa also contained a strong dissenting opinion. Three of the judges claimed that the limitation of fees would permit defendants to pay any rate for counsel, while plaintiffs could not even pay the fair market rate. Accordingly, this would make it difficult for plaintiffs to obtain competent legal representation, which is a constitutional guarantee.

Another issue is whether caps on attorney's fees set by state law would apply in a federal claim under the Federal Torts Claim Act (FTCA). In *Jackson v. United States* (9th Cir.1989), the court held that state law would apply to the extent necessary to establish the substantive liability of the government. Finding a conflict between the limits set by state law and those in the FTCA, the court held that the amount of the attorney's fees had no relationship to the substantive law. Thus, the

FTCA preempted state law with respect to attorney's fees.

D. STATUTORY RATE FREEZE ON MALPRACTICE PREMIUMS

A final method of addressing the malpractice insurance crisis has been through direct control or restriction of rate increases on malpractice premiums. In *Medical Malpractice Joint Underwriting Association of Rhode Island v. Paradis* (D.R.I.1991), the federal district court held that such restrictions on rate increases violate the "takings clause" of the fifth amendment as property of the insurance industry was taken without just compensation. Evidence of this taking was held to be in terms of the accrued deficit that the underwriting fund would incur. Furthermore, the court found that the recoupment methods outlined by the legislature did not allow adequate compensation for the insurers. Thus, at least in that case, the legislative freeze on insurance rates carried the concept of "reform" too far and was held to be unconstitutional.

IV. COUNTERSUITS

In medical malpractice, the countersuit is an action brought by the physician against the patient who previously brought a malpractice suit. The countersuit typically alleges that the malpractice action was brought in bad faith upon a claim that lacked merit, and seeks damages for malicious prosecution, abuse of process or a similar claim. In

Morowitz v. Marvel (D.C.App.1980), two physicians filed suit to collect medical fees owed to them. The patient responded with a countersuit for malpractice, which was subsequently withdrawn. The court held that although abuse of the system is certainly disfavored, would-be litigants with meritorious claims must be provided with free access to the court system. The court held that in order for the physicians to prevail on a claim of malicious prosecution, four separate elements must be pled and proven: (1) The underlying suit was decided in the physician's favor; (2) the defendant showed malice; (3) there was no probable cause for the underlying suit; and (4) special damages were suffered by the plaintiff as a result of the original suit. Special damages are those beyond which would necessarily be expected by anyone involved in a lawsuit. Thus even "professional defamatory type" damages must be expected in this type of suit, and therefore do not qualify as "special damages". This latter element, which is not required in most jurisdictions, may be difficult to satisfy; such difficulty proved to be fatal to the claim in *Morowitz*.

A second important issue addressed in *Morowitz* is whether a suit for malicious prosecution may be brought against the attorney or the plaintiff for a frivolous action. California specifically rejects the idea that counsel would be liable due to the absence of privity of contract or status as an intended beneficiary, as well as public policy concerns. Illinois, which also rejects countersuits against the attorney, adds the rationale that to do so would create an "insurmountable conflict of interest between the attorney and client." *Berlin v. Nathan* (Ill.App. 1978). Finally, New York has reached the same conclusion on the basis that "[w]hatever may be the constraints imposed by the Code of Professional Responsibility with the associated sanctions of professional discipline when baseless legal proceedings are instituted by a lawyer on behalf of a client, the courts have not recognized any liability of the lawyer to third parties . . ." *Drago v. Buonagurio* (N.Y.Ct.App.1978).

Countersuits raise another interesting dilemma. What if a physician, wary of a malpractice action, waits for the tort statute of limitation to expire before filing suit for an unpaid fee? The contract statute of limitation is generally larger than the tort statute, so a collection action may be instituted without fear of triggering a malpractice counterclaim. Three possibilities exist: (1) the collection action could go forward as intended with the malpractice action barred by the statute of limitations; (2) the malpractice action could proceed on the basis that instituting the contract claim implicitly waived the tort statute; or (3) the malpractice action would be precluded, except that poor delivery of medical care could still be a defense to an action seeking to recover the fee for such care.

INDEX

†